Praise for *Choosing Light: Transforming Grief through the Practice of Mindful Photography and Self-Reflection*

"Dr. Thomas presents a fresh, innovative, and impactful vision for the use of mindful photography in processing loss and grief. This book provides an extraordinary new set of tools for counselors and individuals that creates an intersection between psychology, spirituality, and art."

—Terri Daniel, DMin, CT, end-of-life advisor, interfaith chaplaincy, bereavement, and trauma support

"*Choosing Light* offers a gentle invitation to those who are stepping into the realm of grief to slow down and find anchors of connection and support. Grief is disorienting, and most are left wondering what to think, feel, and do. In the pages of this book, those who are grieving and those who support them will find not a prescription, but options for what we might do in and with our grief."

—Jana DeCristofaro, LCSW, community response program coordinator, Dougy Center; host, *Grief Out Loud* podcast

"I am pleased to recommend Dr. Jessica Thomas's *Choosing Light: Transforming Grief through the Practice of Mindful Photography and Self-Reflection*. I come to this having worked with her and the innovative study she completed on her PhD dissertation on this same topic at the Institute of Transpersonal Psychology in 2016. She has continued to explore and develop her project in ways that make what she has done in the field of psychotherapy and contemplative photography even more profound and relevant to the needs of a broader public. I am especially pleased to see how her project has evolved to include ways photographs help facilitate personal growth through ongoing bonds with departed loved ones."

—Mark Gonnerman, MDiv, PhD, former PhD program chair and professor, Institute of Transpersonal Psychology

"In a dominant culture so uncomfortable with death, where ancestral mourning rituals are long forgotten, creative practices like the mindful photography and reflection skillfully taught by Jessica Thomas can offer a transformative portal to meaning-making and healing. I engaged in this practice, with Jessica's support, while mourning the illness and death of a close friend; it helped me slow down, notice the beauty, shed some tears, and think about life and death in fresh ways."

—Holly J. Pruett, funeral celebrant, death doula, community death educator

"Contemplative photography, or mindful photography, is a series of methods for letting go of discursive fixation and releasing into the vividness of direct experience. It is also a way of expressing that vividness to others. Entering into direct experience creates space in the mind for perceptions, feelings, and emotions to be accommodated and recognized. In *Choosing Light*, Jessica Thomas puts these powerful methods to use to help people deal with the great challenges of death, grief, and loss. I commend this important effort."

—Andy Karr, teacher, photographer, and author of *Contemplating Reality: A Practitioner's Guide to the View in Indo-Tibetan Buddhism*

"Dr. Thomas's masterful writing about the practice of mindful photography and reflective journaling benefits people who grieve and those who sit alongside them. Her words are a gift, which when opened, empowers the reader to uncover and make meaning out of often hidden, mysterious layers of personal feelings around death. Viewing the shared images makes readers' hearts swell with emotion. This book is an awakening that is good for the soul."

—Susan L. Schoenbeck, nurse educator; author of *Good Grief: Daily Meditations: A Book of Caring and Remembrance*

CHOOSING LIGHT

Transforming Grief through the Practice of Mindful Photography and Self-Reflection

JESSICA N. THOMAS, LMFT, PhD

ROWMAN & LITTLEFIELD
Lanham • Boulder • New York • London

Published by Rowman & Littlefield
An imprint of The Rowman & Littlefield Publishing Group, Inc.
4501 Forbes Boulevard, Suite 200, Lanham, Maryland 20706
www.rowman.com

86-90 Paul Street, London EC2A 4NE

British Library Cataloguing in Publication Information available

Library of Congress Cataloging-in-Publication Data
Names: Thomas, Jessica N., author.
Title: Choosing light : transforming grief through the practice of mindful photography and
  self-reflection / Jessica N. Thomas, LMFT, PhD.
Description: Lanham : Rowman & Littlefield, [2024] | Includes bibliographical references and
  index.
Identifiers: LCCN 2024003658 (print) | LCCN 2024003659 (ebook) | ISBN 9781538193181
  (cloth) | ISBN 9781538193198 (paperback) | ISBN 9781538193204 (epub)
Subjects: LCSH: Grief. | Photography--Psychological aspects. | Mindfulness (Psychology) |
  Self-confidence.
Classification: LCC BF575.G7 T486 2024 (print) | LCC BF575.G7 (ebook) | DDC 155.9/37–
  dc23/eng/20240318
LC record available at https://lccn.loc.gov/2024003658
LC ebook record available at https://lccn.loc.gov/2024003659

♾️™ The paper used in this publication meets the minimum requirements of American National Standard for Information Sciences—Permanence of Paper for Printed Library Materials, ANSI/ NISO Z39.48-1992.

For Francine, my shining light

CONTENTS

FOREWORD

When someone we love dies, many people believe that their soul embarks on a great journey. In my work, I have seen that equally, for those who are the bereaved, there is an immense and lonely journey. The relational-mirror is shattered and in the journey of grief, we who are bereaved walk among those shards, to mend a new world into being. Upon the death of a loved one, an infinite crevasse opens up in our world—actually, it is an aspect of consciousness which has opened up, and the psyche offers both terror and beauty at such transformative times.

In the words of the poet David Whyte, "Beauty is the harvest of presence, the evanescent moment of seeing or hearing on the outside what already lives far inside us."

Beauty replaces that lost relational-mirror with another lens, the harvest of presence, so that what is beheld as an inner vision can be glimpsed, however briefly, on the outside. Through mindful photography, one is seeing so clearly that one is transformed in the seeing and then transmitting that moment to others. Art has great potential energy, the energy that changes personal and societal realities. The key is to pay attention.

As Henri Cartier-Bresson, the renowned photographer, put it: "People think far too much about techniques and not enough about seeing." The sensitivity of this instrument to the photographer's seeing facilitates the therapeutic process: the camera is adept enough to receive that vital impulse which is the vividness of personal vision and transpose it to paper. And the deep well of grief provides, to the photographic process, a point of view that enables it to show life its own image, reflected in those waters. For instance, Thomas describes the photo made by Judy, a caregiver for her dying friend, who contrasts the dark of a mirror with the light of the natural world—she noticed, in that moment, how life is reflected back to us by the presence of death. Her image captures, perfectly, how the entirety of life is reflected and magnified by mortality. In this double mirror—that of caregiver Judy's image and that of author Jessica's recounting of this experience—I am reminded of a poem by Rainer Maria Rilke.

In Rilke's "Requiem for a Friend," written for the painter Paula Modersohn-Becker, he writes, "artists in their work sometimes intuit that they must keep transforming, where they love," commending her for having nurtured a growing edge that was visible in her personal and creative work. Rilke would agree with Jessica Thomas that art-making is a ritual, an embodied narrative, that facilitates the flow of love and transformation. As with Thomas's participant Judy, the art-making has revealed Paula's inner awareness, made it visible—this clear seeing and creativity, which has borne fruit through both art-making and through childbirth—an awareness now transposed to his poem. As a result, her interior vision is mirrored back and amplified. That vision now, by virtue of being established within these pages, finds a wider community and, thus, another source of generativity. She is granted a kind of immortality through his poem. This "saturation of awareness" is what photographer Cedric Wright believed gave rise to great art, which was then "permeated with an inner perception of beauty and an inner personal philosophy." Rilke had *chosen light* by looking at grief rather than staying in the dark of denial—he willingly entered into that transformation, and it was creatively advantageous. Rilke experienced a breakthrough when writing "Requiem for a Friend," which propelled him to write the *Duino Elegies*, *Sonnets to Orpheus*, and other masterpieces—the near presence of death served to facilitate his own artistic process so that he was able to hold a mirror up to the mysteries of love and transformation that are uncovered through the human journey.

In the mindful photography process, this act of creation similarly illuminates the art of departure and arrival, that single movement which is both in-breath and out-breath—the miracle of which becomes apparent through the contemplative pause. Through that granting of inner space, we see, as Zen Master Eihei Dōgen remarked, "This birth-and-death is the life of a buddha."

It is our hope that Jessica Thomas's book helps others to find solace and meaning-making through the process of mindful photography described here. Mindful photography is a sacred ritual that discovers the sacred within the ordinary through paying attention: When we see clearly, we are in contact with the mysteries of love and transformation and illuminate for others the beauty that can be glimpsed only along this path of being mortal.

Ji Hyang Padma, Ph.D.

Acknowledgments

I wish to acknowledge and give thanks to my husband, Aaron, for his unending support, care, and love. Thank you to my extended family: your presence in my life is a blessing that I cherish dearly. In times of joy, you have celebrated with me wholeheartedly, and in moments of challenge, you offered your encouragement and wisdom. Each one of you has played a unique role in shaping who I am today. Your kindness and unconditional love have taught me the true meaning of family and have enriched my life in countless ways. I am forever thankful for the memories we've created and the lessons I've learned from each of you. Gratitude to my best friend of over thirty-five years, muse and mindful photographer Jennifer Kulka. Your passion for photography opened my eyes to the beauty that surrounds us every day. Your creativity knows no bounds, and your ability to capture the essence of a moment with your camera never fails to leave me in awe. A special thank you to Ali Shaw at Indigo Editing: Your expertise, dedication, and keen eye for detail have been instrumental in bringing this project to fruition.

Lastly, endless gratitude to all those who participated in my research study and generously shared their experiences and practices for this book. Your willingness to participate and share your insights has been invaluable in shaping the content and depth of this work. Your contributions have enriched the narrative and provided valuable perspectives that will undoubtedly be a catalyst for healing for other readers.

INTRODUCTION

In my twenties, I lost two people close to me, my father and my grandmother, but I experienced those losses in very different ways. Those close losses and the grief experiences that followed changed me and led me to study death and dying and write this book. I was moved to revisit these losses when I came across an old journal years later at the family house.

My father's death was totally traumatic for me. It was unexpected, and I was only twenty-one. He died of an accidental overdose of prescribed pain medication. Five years prior to his death, he had fallen off a ladder at work and had a back and knee injury. Over the years, the pain grew, and he ended up having chronic pain. He was seeing several doctors, but none of them could effectively help him manage his pain outside of prescribing more pain medications. The night my father died, I was staying at my parents' home because I was having dental work done early the next morning. I came home late that night, and I wanted to check in with my mother because she was to drive me the next morning to get my wisdom teeth out. When I knocked on my parents' bedroom door to wake her up, I called, "Hey, what time are we to leave in the morning?"

When she got up, at some point, she touched my father and discovered that he was cold. She started yelling for me to come in. My brother, who happened to be downstairs, came running up and tried to perform CPR. Everything happened extremely fast.

When the emergency medical technicians arrived, they actually zipped my father up in a body bag in front of the family, which was totally thoughtless and traumatic for me. After that, I had a visual memory of that devastating event. I had a clear image of my father's face in that black bag and the zipper being pulled over him. I couldn't erase that image from my mind for a long time.

As I was reading through my old journal, I came across this entry:

> A year later, and I feel more lonely and sad than ever. I just cry and cry all alone. Not once did I cry at his rosary or funeral. Not once did I express any pain to my family over the past year. But, suddenly now, when everyone seems to be feeling better, I feel worse than ever. The timing seems very wrong. Is this how things will continue to happen to me—at the wrong time? Does anything ever happen at the right time? I don't know. Is there a reason for this that I don't see right now?

I could not fathom there not being meaning in such a tragic event. It was interesting to me that I wanted, and perhaps on some level needed, some sort of meaning to come from that experience. Reflecting on the journal entries that I wrote about the loss of my father, I realized that I was stuck in a place of words and ruminating on words without inviting other parts of my experience—visual imagery, creative expression, and embodiment. I also realized the sense of helplessness that I had internalized. The sense that something terrible had been done to me and I had no control and zero choices.

I wrote about feeling isolated. I didn't have any friends who could relate to having lost a parent, and so, for some time after the funeral, I felt a dark lull and very isolated with my emotions. My father had a fun-loving personality, which added a lot of light to the family. He loved to make jokes and listen to good music. He was also very spiritual and existential. The light that he so naturally carried for the family was suddenly extinguished—and the entire family system was impacted by that. I felt trapped in the sadness of that loss for a long time—just zipped up. Other entries reflected my curiosity regarding time and my capacity to be present or escape grief. As I revisited those journal entries, I thought about how different the grief process of losing my father was versus the grief process with my grandmother that took place seven years after my father's death. With my father's death, I wanted so badly to escape the pain and suffering that grew from having lost him so suddenly. I grappled with the conflicting ideas of escaping my grief or choosing to be present.

> So much of the time, I find myself fixated on the next moment, the next day, the next week, the next month, or even next year. But what about this moment, today? It's difficult to stay in this moment, right now. How do I escape my pain? Or, how do I choose to be with it here in this moment?

The second major loss was my grandmother's death, and that death was strikingly different from my father's death. It was timely and expected and a death that I was able to be present for. Our family had the opportunity to take care of her, talk to her, and observe the dying process. We came together during this time and felt a sense of safety, connection, purpose, and meaning.

I was raised in a multigenerational household, so my grandmother was like a third parent to me in many ways. Because both of my parents worked full-time, my grandmother cared for my brother and me as we were growing up. As a homemaker, she was always there for us. At the age of ninety-six, she was admitted to the hospital for congestive heart failure. Soon after, when the doctors decided she wasn't going to get any better, my mother, my brother, and I decided to bring her home to die, and I moved back into the family home to help take care of her. For about a year, I would wake up in the morning, make us both breakfast, and check on her throughout the day. What I was doing for her mirrored many things that she had done for me, and so I felt a sense of giving back, which gave me a great deal of joy and purpose.

Grandma was a tough woman. She was born in 1913 and grew up in western Kansas and was the oldest female of eight children, all of whom had worked on the family farm. As I was growing up, she taught me to garden. She really liked hard labor and working outside. In her eighties, she was still carrying cement blocks across the yard. She was a very practical and determined person. The combination of her physical and mental strength lent itself, I think, to her aging well and dying well. I would say that she died consciously. She knew that she was dying and was able to reflect on that fact with a sense of peace and acceptance.

During the last day of her life, my grandmother was totally present mentally. We talked about stories from the farm in Claflin, Kansas, we prayed for her future, and conversed deeply about the present. That evening, we talked about those family members and friends who had already made their journey from this world and how she might see them again.

I stayed over that night, sitting at her bedside. Just after midnight, I could tell by her breathing and the resting lull in the room that the end was approaching. I woke my mother, who was sleeping next door, and said, "You know, I think you want to go in there. I think we're at the end." When my mother joined me in my grandmother's bedroom, she agreed that this was likely the end. Although Grandma's breathing was labored, her eyes were open, and she was looking at me with a watery gaze.

We each held one of Grandma's hands as we meditatively chanted the rosary. It was very different from when I had prayed the rosary aloud in church growing up. The energy in Grandma's room was peaceful, as if time were standing still. Every moment, every second, was slowed down. Then she took her last breath, and that was the end. That was the most peaceful energy I have ever experienced—very different from the shock of my father's passing. Earlier that day, my brother had brought his six-month-old baby, Anthony, over to say hello—and, as it happened, also goodbye. When the baby was propped up on the bed with her, I saw their hands next to each other. My nephew's smooth little, young hand, contrasting with my grandmother's aged, wrinkled, discolored hand, was striking for me. In fact, it was so striking that I got my camera and made an image. (Photo 0.1) I saw the whole human lifespan right there in those hands. The image I made captured a moment of my experience that reflected a deep shift in my being. As time passed, this picture became a kind of spiritual guide for me, keeping the deeply felt shift alive. This image never fails to ground me spiritually; it is an anchor that reconnects me with compassion, love, and wisdom.

The loss I felt from my grandmother's death was very different from the delayed grief I experienced seven years earlier with my father's death, which had been so unexpected and traumatic. An important difference is

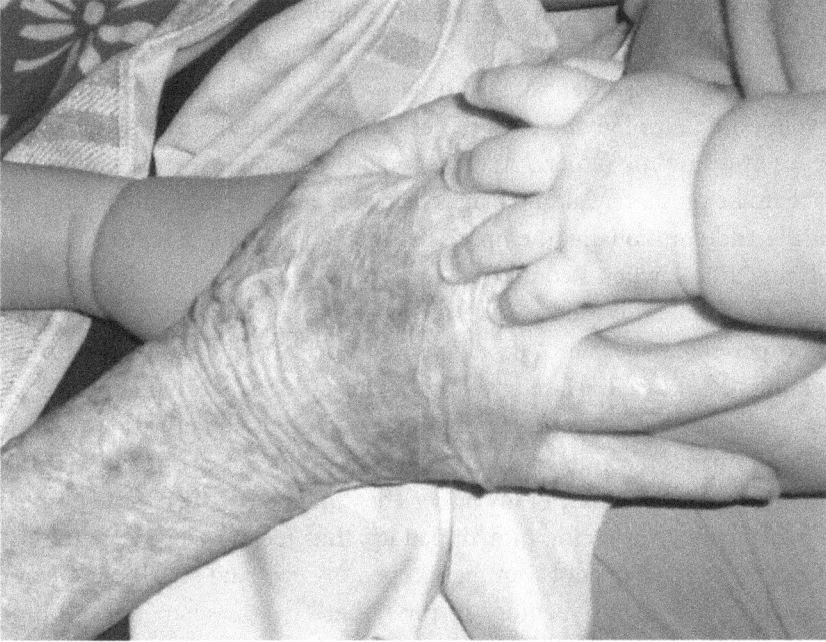

Photo 0.1. Jessica, hands. Photo courtesy of author.

that I was *confronted* by my father's death and only *faced* it later. I hadn't even begun to process my father's death until a year later when I cried for him for the first time. Somehow, I had switched my emotions off because I had been too shocked and had no tools to process my grief. Seeing my father zipped up in a body bag had given me a sense that *I* had been zipped up. Or I had zipped myself up. I couldn't emotionally open myself to the process. That visual memory was symbolic for me.

I didn't cry once at my father's funeral. In the afternoon after my grandmother's death, while my family was in the living room, I was sitting in my grandmother's rocking chair, and suddenly, I started crying in front of everyone. I really let my guard down, and that was a highly significant moment for me. I was open and didn't feel zipped up or stuck. I believe that moment spoke to my capacity to be open and present through the loss of my grandmother. I allowed myself to be open as opposed to how closed I had been with my father.

With my grandmother, I had more time to move through the grief process. I had the opportunity to face my grandmother's death on my own terms, at a slower pace, starting even before she died. Having that wonderful year of giving back to her helped to heal the traumatic experience of losing my father. I really savored the moments with her and was able to be present. Making images helped me be present both psychologically and emotionally; it empowered me and gave me a sense of agency during a time when I could have easily shut down emotionally.

The camera, I believe, helps us to be present and open to all kinds of experiences. Certainly, it helped me to be mindfully present with my grandmother in those last days, keeping my eyes open through the process of death and loss. Beyond making images, there is the process of reflecting on images. For me, repeated reflection on images created an imprint in my mind. In the case of my father's death, I repeatedly returned to that visual memory of seeing him zipped up, thus feeling zipped up and not wanting to open up, not wanting to open my eyes and see. The traumatic image etched in my memory of my father's death versus the inspiring image involving mindful photography with my grandmother's death, albeit both powerful, stimulated different results. Repeated reflection on the image of my grandmother and nephew's hands became a catalyst for my spiritual growth and development as it continued to inspire hope. Days, months, and years later, I returned to that photograph, and every time I did, it gave me a sense of pure compassion, gratitude, and peace as it reconnected me to that experience of letting go. That image reminds me of the regeneration of life and the hope that is always present when we choose to see it.

Imagery is a vital part of all the stories we create. Being able to be present and open our eyes to what is happening is important, and the camera can help us to do that. It can help us to engage the moment and be present for what is happening right in front of us, particularly in difficult times. Making images mindfully and reflecting on those images through journaling can create a sense of wholeness in the meaning-making process. For myself, one without the other seemed incomplete.

From a young age, I was death curious. I grew up in a large family system where death was not hidden. I can remember visiting great aunts and uncles and family friends before they died. Attending funerals for family, friends, and community members who died was, in some ways, like attending a wedding. So, even before the life-altering losses of my father and grandmother, death was another part of life. That said, honoring the deaths of peripheral family and friends is different than losing an attachment figure. Being death curious did not mitigate my being grief-stricken from my father's death. However, I do believe my curiosity helped my grief process in that I was drawn to reflect on my experience. Through that reflective process, my curiosity, creativity, and passion grew. All those pieces, including the longing and sadness and angst, alchemized—rendering a transformative process.

My personal experiences of grief and loss inspired me to work professionally with others who found themselves in the midst of unwanted change and difficult life transitions. I began my work as a systemic therapist working with veterans in a PTSD clinic and with those who were traversing grief and loss due to death, houselessness, or the foster care system, as well as for those who had a role as a caregiver. I integrated photographs and photographic reflection into therapy sessions early on, starting with my work at a university therapy clinic. However, it wasn't until I was working with teens in the foster care system that I paired mindful photography and photo reflection together as a therapeutic technique. It was through this meaningful work that I began to see and understand its powerful impact of stimulating curiosity, creativity, and empowerment.

Meanwhile, my passion for understanding end-of-life transitions grew as I continued to reflect on the experience I had with my grandmother and through my volunteer work with hospice. I was inspired to pursue my doctoral studies in transpersonal psychology because of its emphasis on psycho-spiritual development and how the connection between the self and higher consciousness can lead to transformative growth.

Initially, I wrote a research proposal on mindfulness and caregiving, but I felt deeply that something was missing. I was conflicted, but like most things in life, if you give them a little time and space, answers can surface. While on a flight, I was reading chapter 4 of *The Tibetan Book of the Dead* titled "Natural Liberation through Naked Perception." At one point, I looked up from my page and gazed out the airplane window and into the open sky and clouds. Suddenly, the image I'd made of my grandmother's and nephew's hands flashed in my mind. I knew right away that the missing piece was the imagery and practice that allowed me to be so present and mindful. This was the genesis of the Within and Without Mindful Photography Method.

I truly believe the potential for transformation is within us all—we are creative beings! Something extraordinary can transpire when we are able to be mindfully present and reflect on our grief experiences. I hope this book awakens you to the transformative aspects of grief. Learning to slow down, notice, create, and reflect on self-made images will inspire a sense of confidence, inner strength, gratitude, meaningful insight, and wisdom through your grief journey. My ultimate hope for you is that this book helps you discover your most precious resources:

- Your capacity to confront and reflect on difficult things, such as grief
- Your innate creative and imaginative potential
- Your ability to derive meaning from your own creations and experiences
- Your capacity to grow and transform through grief

CHAPTER 1

Reflecting on Death, Grief, and Loss

The call of death is a call of love. Death can be sweet if we answer it in the affirmative, if we accept it as one of the great eternal forms of life and transformation.

—HESSE, H.

TO EXPERIENCE DEATH IS TO EXPERIENCE LIFE. WHEN WE EXPERIENCE death through losing a loved one or by watching someone we care about decline, we confront the nature of impermanence. When my father passed away unexpectedly, I felt overwhelmed and needed time to sort through my feelings. Perhaps you feel anxious, angry, shocked, confused, depressed, or even relieved. There is no right way to grieve. Whatever your feelings might be in the moment, they are a human response to having loved and lost. However difficult our grief process might be, it is how we choose to proceed in the wake of suffering that can shape us.

Facing mortality, whether it be your own death or a close friend or family member, might bring about an epiphany that awakens you to the importance of healing old wounds and reordering priorities for deeper and more meaningful relationships. Death is a transformational process and can create ripe conditions to cultivate deep compassion while expanding awareness and a sense of responsibility beyond ourselves. When my grandmother died, I had the opportunity to connect with her on a deeper level, using the time she had left to care for her with compassion and hear stories about her life.

Human experiences can be difficult, evoking pain, suffering, loneliness, fear, and ambiguity. By acknowledging pain, we develop a greater appreciation for the beauty of life. Death and loss are inextricably linked to the existential and spiritual nature of life. Death of a loved one or anticipating the death of a loved one can be a catastrophic event, throwing us into an open sea of ambiguous emotion. Through reflection on death, grief, loss, and impermanence, we are faced with our own mortality and have to wrestle with existential and spiritual questions. Although working through these questions can be challenging, this process also offers opportunities for growth. Our connection to life is measured in part by our connection to death and acceptance of the impermanent nature of life. Sogyal Rinpoche, a Buddhist monk, describes this process beautifully:

> Life is nothing but a continuing dance of birth and death, dance of change. Every time I hear the rush of a mountain stream, or the waves crashing on the mountain shore, or my own heartbeat, I hear the sound of impermanence. These changes, these small deaths, are our living links to death. They are death's pulse, death's heartbeat, prompting us to let go of all the things we cling to.
>
> So let us then work with these changes now, in life: that is the real way to prepare for death. Life may be full of pain, suffering, and difficulty, but all of these are opportunities handed to us to help us move toward an emotional acceptance of death. It is only when we believe things to be permanent that we shut off the possibility of learning from change.

It's important to acknowledge that no grief experience is the same. Each death experience is marked by numerous qualities, some of which are more complex than others. An example of this is the striking difference in my own experiences that I discussed in the introduction regarding the complicated loss of my father versus the anticipated loss of my grandmother. Albeit both transformational, they were very different grief journeys. Another point worth highlighting is the way that one grief experience might inform the next grief experience, and so on and so forth. Because I had suffered such a traumatic and complicated loss with my father and never got the chance to tell him goodbye, it was very important for me to be present throughout my grandmother's death and savor those last moments with her.

As you think about circumstances related to your own grief journey, I recommend reflecting on your experiences with self-compassion in mind. Self-compassion is helpful through grief because it reminds us of our humanity and our ability to be kind to ourselves in the midst of suffering. It also introduces the practice of mindfulness because we must be present with our experiences and emotions to offer ourselves kindness and compassion. Like the friend who turns away at the first sign of a tear, if you can't be present with your own grief, then how can you acknowledge it, offer yourself understanding, and move forward into the meaning-making journey of grief and loss? Self-compassion has three core components: self-kindness, common humanity, and mindfulness.

- Self-kindness simply means caring about ourselves and being willing to take wise action to alleviate our suffering.
- Common humanity is recognizing that all humans experience suffering. Even though the details differ, all humans face grief and loss and vulnerability and failure. And we are all doing the best we can, given the circumstances of our life. This common humanity piece is what differentiates self-compassion from self-pity.
- Mindfulness is about the ability to relate to our experience with a sense of balance or equanimity, a calm and clear mind—even when it feels like the rug has been pulled out from under us. We can be okay with the messy nature of grief—and let go of our expectations that things be any different than exactly as they are.

It can be challenging to hold your grief with compassion, particularly if you live within systems where grief is dismissed or denied. Grievers can worry that they are grieving incorrectly, or that it is taking too long, or they might dwell on the things they should or shouldn't have done. These kinds of thoughts and feelings might surface in the time leading up to a loss as one anticipates the death of a loved one or after a death has occurred. Complicated feelings can arise, such as regret, guilt, shame, or even self-blame, that further exacerbate the grief process.

If you can meet these thoughts and feelings with kindness and compassion, you can soften their edges. Pema Chödrön, a Tibetan Buddhist nun and author, has written extensively on grief, loss, and compassion. She reminds us that the way we relate to our experiences can cause suffering: "It isn't the things that happen to us in our lives that cause us to suffer, it's how we relate to the things that happen to us that causes us to suffer." In other words, clinging to unkind and critical thoughts and stories about your grief can perpetuate suffering.

If you can hold your grief with a sense of compassion, you can move through difficult thoughts and feelings without clinging to them or denying them. Instead of overidentifying with them, you can acknowledge them as part of a larger journey. As you reflect on your own journey of grief and loss—whether it's anticipatory grief, complicated grief, or any other kind of grief—I encourage you to pause and gently acknowledge those thoughts and feelings with a sense of kindness and knowledge that they are, in fact, there because you are human, not because you are weak or because you are doing something wrong.

ANTICIPATORY GRIEF

Anticipatory grief is an emotional response that is experienced before a loss, occurring when there is an impending death. It is sometimes overlooked as an actual grief experience, even though it can be as intense as the grief that follows the death of a loved one. This is what I experienced as I cared for my grandmother and prepared for her passing. I found myself wanting to hold on to every moment, every memory, knowing her time with our family was ending soon.

Anticipatory grief is sometimes an unconscious process that happens when stability is threatened, most often by an unwelcomed diagnosis. It encompasses the mourning, coping, and planning of one's life in response to an impending loss as well as future losses. Losses might include loss of function and mobility, loss of identity, and changes in roles, in addition to loss of life. For instance, losing your ability to dress yourself or cook for yourself—or watching these changes in your loved one—is part of the grief process.

A challenging dynamic that I hear about frequently is the role reversal that happens when a parent begins to decline and the adult child begins caregiving tasks. These kinds of shifts in roles can trigger difficult feelings and relational dynamics. All of these losses accumulate along the progression of an illness as anticipatory grief processes continue to be triggered. The result can be an overwhelming feeling of loss.

Anticipatory grief can be experienced not only by the terminally ill person but also by family, friends, and caregivers. Someone who has just received difficult news about their cancer diagnosis may begin to show signs of anticipatory grief. You may feel anxious, sad, helpless, disorganized, forgetful, or angry. Doubting your faith and questioning your belief system is also a common experience while anticipating a death. People may also notice difficulty in connecting emotionally with others. However difficult anticipating a loss might be, the experience can also be beneficial in that you have time to prepare and develop coping skills for the changes to come. I certainly found this to be true as I cared for my grandmother. Having that time with her allowed me to confront and process the loss with her. As I assisted with everyday caregiving tasks and moments of connection with her, I became emotionally and psychologically prepared for her death.

As humans, we have the capacity to look to the future. We anticipate with fear and hope, and oftentimes, we find ourselves oscillating between the two. When we are faced with the loss of a loved one (or a major life transition), we might find ourselves ruminating with fear: we fear living without our loved one, we fear what life might be like without them, or we fear never being happy again, and perhaps we fear loneliness. On the other hand, we also have hope. We hope that our loved one will be free from pain and suffering, we hope for a cure to their disease or illness, we hope we will be able to learn and grow from the experience, and we believe that healing is possible.

Anticipating loss and change offers fertile ground for using what might be one of our greatest resources—the capacity to be present and create meaning even in the most difficult of times, such as before the death of a loved one has happened. Such was the case for me as I cared for my grandmother when she was dying. In those last few days of her life, I found myself frequently oscillating between fear and hope. I feared not being ready for her death and losing my chance to experience a meaningful goodbye. I hoped that I could be strong in the days to come so that I might be present for her and my family. Unlike after my father's death, which was so sudden, I knew I had an opportunity to mentally and emotionally prepare by being with her and making time to reflect on my feelings along the way.

Bringing awareness to anticipatory loss and learning ways to enhance our ability to cultivate inner strength, gratitude, insight, and wisdom can prepare us to move through these difficult times with greater ease, while also positioning us to grow from the experience of loss. Being psychologically and emotionally prepared can bring about feelings of peace for both your loved one who is dying and their greater community of friends, family, and caregivers.

COMPLICATED GRIEF

Grief might feel more complicated after the loss of a child, a life partner, or a sudden death by violent means. People who have faced multiple losses close together, a traumatic loss, an unexpected or untimely loss, and those who do not have community support or time and space to process their feelings might also experience grief that feels intense and complicated. It is important to know that this form of grief is a natural response to the death of a loved one and is not pathological.

Perhaps the most poignant characteristics of complicated grief are intense yearning, longing, and sadness. These experiences are usually accompanied by unrelenting thoughts or images of the person who has died and a sense of disbelief or an inability to accept the painful reality of the loss. You might find yourself thinking about how you might have prevented the death or how someone else might have prevented the death. This kind of guilt and anger is common, in particular for those who attempted CPR on a loved one or lost someone to suicide. Ruminations about such thoughts and feelings can quickly become internalized beliefs as our brains try to make sense of difficult and traumatic experiences.

I experienced a deep sense of abandonment in the wake of my father's death. When the loss is a parent, child, best friend, or life partner, grief can feel like an attachment wound—an emotional injury that is characterized by a feeling of abandonment or betrayal during a critical moment of need.[1] These kinds of losses are complicated because the very person you might normally reach out to in times of distress is the same person who is not present to offer you connection and support, further contributing to your distress.

As living beings, we enter the world with a vital need for attachment security from cradle to grave. Our emotions, physiology, sense of well-being, and contact with our inner and outer worlds depend a lot on the relationships we have with people. While this need to connect is hardwired into our embodied neural system for survival, that same wiring leaves us vulnerable to devastating distress when we lose the very beings who offer support and give our lives a sense of security and meaning. Because attachment relationships are so vital to us, the permanent loss of those we love can affect us on the deepest level. Our emotions can feel intense and overwhelming.

People sometimes grow ashamed of their intense grief. It is important to practice self-compassion and reach out for support and community so we better understand the complexities of grief, accept the reality of death, and re-envision a future. Creative rituals and practices, such as mindful photography, can offer a path through intense grief and inspire a healing journey forward.

PREPAREDNESS

Being prepared for death can lead to more positive bereavement outcomes and help us grow spiritually. Awareness, acceptance, and meaning-making are key contributors to a shift in existential and spiritual perceptions.[2] Becoming aware of impermanence and learning about death can prepare you for the inevitable loss of loved ones, positioning you to cultivate meaning and gain spiritual insight through loss.

Being unprepared for the death of a loved one is associated with increased depression, anxiety, and a more complicated grief process.[3] This was certainly evident for me as I reflected on the striking difference in the grief I felt after the sudden death of my father versus the grief I felt while I anticipated the death of my grandmother. Increased awareness of death and being prepared emotionally, mentally, existentially, and spiritually can usher in acceptance of the loss, making the experience more meaningful.

Opening our eyes and hearts to death and loss and choosing to be mindfully present through the grief process engages the most authentic parts of ourselves. Our meaningful presence with a dying loved one and those reflective moments we create for ourselves become a path forward through the impending fear of death and loss. As we prepare for loss, we notice our interconnectedness—and within those heartfelt moments, we recognize the essence of who we are, nourishing our inner strength.

Confronting impermanence through grief presents an opportunity for profound growth and a new appreciation for life. While in the throes of grief, however, you might struggle to recognize such an opportunity. Experiences with death and loss have the power to pave a path toward discovering your most precious internal resources, such as the following:

- Your capacity to confront and reflect on difficult things, such as death
- Your innate creative and imaginative potential
- Your ability to derive meaning from your own creations and experiences
- Your capacity to grow and transform through grief

An important thing to remember is that grief is a part of being human. It is a normal response of living and loving. Avoiding grief and loss also means avoiding a life filled with love. No matter how hard life can be, we can make a decision to live fully, defining who we are and how we choose to work through grief.

As I shared in the introduction, mindful photography helped me stay present when I was caregiving for my grandmother. It helped me be aware of my thoughts and feelings and gave me the inner strength to process them. Rather than avoiding or dismissing the challenging aspects of watching my loved one decline, I could acknowledge those challenges.

Furthermore, I could engage more fully and see other aspects of my experience beyond sadness, fear, and angst.

The Within and Without Method outlined in this book can assist you in working through the complexities of grief and loss. The cultivation of internal resources, such as courage, gratitude, and wisdom, can help you be present through grief rather than resisting and avoiding it. Through this transformative lens, there can be a shift in the way you hold grief in your life—rather than grieving being something that happens to you, you can choose how you grieve. Rather than falling victim to your circumstances, you accept challenges, move through them, and learn from them. This is how grief can transform your life and help you uncover a well of internal resources you did not know existed.

NOTES

1. Holmes, 2014.

2. Cacciatore and Flint, 2012; Currier, Holland, and Neimeyer, 2006; Rushton et al., 2009.

3. Hebert et al., 2006; Lobb et al., 2010.

CHAPTER 2

Expanding Awareness

*Grief shakes us loose from our spiritual lethargy and creates a wound
that is far more than a wound. It is an opening to a higher awareness
that can lead to greater peace in life, and also in death.*

- TERRI DANIEL

WHEN YOU ENCOUNTER DEATH, THE IDEA OF NO LONGER EXISTING SUDdenly becomes real. Overwhelming feelings and complex thoughts can flood your mind and body, leaving you entrenched in complete and utter turmoil. Experiencing the depths of disappointment, sorrow, and grief supports your movement into existential being. Finding clarity through the fog of ambivalence is an essential stage that leads to transpersonal understanding and spiritual growth. Contemplating concepts like attachment, impermanence, and death can transform your perspective. Death is universal and often leads the way in cultivating deep compassion and connection with all life forms. Being mindfully aware of the process of loss can help you look and see more deeply into your experience, uncovering profound opportunities for healing and growth.

MINDFULNESS
The term *mindfulness* has its roots in the Pali word *sati*, meaning awareness, attention, and remembering. Cognitive behaviorists have said that it is the relationships we create among our thoughts that cause challenges and not the thoughts themselves that lead to suffering. The historic

Buddha had the same realization while sitting under the Bodhi tree over 2,600 years ago, the night he attained enlightenment. "He saw that all that arises also passes away." "Right mindfulness," one aspect of the Buddha's golden rules for attaining enlightenment, often referred to as the Noble Eightfold Path, is considered foundational to all other steps on the path.[1] Mindfulness is defined as fostering the capacity for "right view," that is, a view not clouded by the everyday confusion of an unrelaxed and ruminative mind.[2]

Mindfulness is an orientation toward our experiences in the present moment characterized by curiosity, openness, and acceptance. This state of self-observation can introduce a space between our perceptions and responses. Orientation to mindfulness begins with making a commitment to maintain an attitude of curiosity about where the mind wanders whenever it inevitably drifts away from the breath, as well as curiosity about the different objects within our experience at any moment. These components work synergistically, enabling you to respond to situations more reflectively, becoming open to the liminal or in-between space and seeing things differently.

Therapeutic qualities of mindfulness in the West first became evident in 1979 through Jon Kabat-Zinn's developing work with an outpatient stress-reduction clinic at the University of Massachusetts Medical Center with a program known as mindfulness-based stress reduction (MBSR). Although mindfulness meditation was conceived by Buddhism, MBSR meditation training was presented as meditation training to mediate pain and stress from medical symptoms. Approaching mindfulness as stress-reduction training, not only a Buddhist meditation practice, made the benefits of mindfulness more accessible to the general public. Mindfulness has since been widely recognized as an effective tool to promote healing through being open with nonjudgmental awareness of the present moment.

In times of loss and pain, our minds tend to disengage, becoming disenfranchised from our experiences, or our thoughts and emotions become so turbulent that we overindulge them. Practicing mindfulness can provide a format for accepting your thoughts and feelings and forming new meaning and understanding of yourself and others. Through my own end-of-life caregiving for my grandmother, hospice volunteer experience, and my research, I observed that in order to experience such a shift in awareness, it helped if my heart and mind were fully engaged and present. This allowed me to become less self-focused, and my pain dissipated as I became aware of the connection and the transpersonal aspects of my experience and identity. Mindfulness, practiced during the sacred time of grief, can create the space that is needed to inspire existential awareness, acceptance, and transformation.

AESTHETIC PERCEPTION

While most aesthetic theories of fine arts focus exclusively on value judgments made by spectators, a mindful approach focuses on thoughts within the imagemaker during the acts of creating and perceiving. A mindful approach to aesthetics is less concerned with objective value of self-made images and more concerned with the intrinsic qualities that are experienced: feeling, perception, and reflection. Feeling is a moment of *resonance* when something in our environment calls forth a gentle invitation to pause and notice.

Feeling and perception give rise to reflection and expression. It is through the body's senses that we perceive the qualities of an experience that prompt meaning-making. When you are on a mindfulness walk, your senses are completely engaged in the experience. Rather than the passive awareness of getting from point A to point B when the purpose is on *getting somewhere*, a mindfulness walk emphasizes process. You are truly engaged in the present moment as you feel your body moving, hear your feet hit the ground, and notice colors, shadows, light, and reflections.

French phenomenological philosopher Maurice Merleau-Ponty emphasized the body as the primary way of knowing the world.[3] He rejected the long philosophical tradition of placing thinking-consciousness as the primary source of knowledge and instead maintained that the body and its perceived world could not be disentangled from each other. It is through your body that you sense and attune with your environment and can perceive your lived experience. Acknowledging your body while grieving is important because it is the miraculous vessel that moves you through the ever-changing landscape of emotions; it is a treasured conduit that can lead you toward the transformational stages of grief. Perception through the body leads to sympathetic reflection through feeling, allowing us to resonate with the aesthetic object.[4] Because aesthetic perception is experienced and not merely grasped objectively, we must be open to receiving and committed to participating through reflection. This implies a mode of being or presence that demands surrender.

Through aesthetic perception, objects can attain existential significance when the imagemaker resonates with them. Feeling is revealed as depth, as a type of knowledge or deeper understanding. Through sympathetic reflection, objects become existentially known. Sympathetic reflection or aesthetic attitude can be described as a silencing of the ego and surrender of the existential self to the sensuous values of our experience and surrounding objects.

Through the practice of mindfulness photography, you engage in sympathetic reflection of the images you create, giving rise to the meaning-making process. For an aesthetic experience to evolve, you must be open to perception with feeling and committed to a process, not merely a means to an end. Mindful photography is not concerned with value judgments such as whether an image is good or bad, ugly or beautiful. More importantly, mindful photography is concerned with process—are you mindfully aware, open, and curious? Did you share a moment of resonance or connection with your environment? Did you answer an invitation from your environment to pause, notice, and create?

Employing sympathetic reflection and the aesthetic attitude in the practice of mindful photography inspires contemplation and meaning-making as you reflect and perceive your creations from a place of feeling and existential awareness and your current lived experiences of facing death, grief, loss, and life transitions.

In my research study in 2016, participants began the practice of mindful photography by becoming attuned to their aesthetic experience. Participants described qualities of their visual field that drew their attention and brought them into the present moment, such as shadows, light, color, texture, and even objects. They became visually attuned as they noticed being drawn to something in their experience that caused them to slow down and foster a sense of curiosity. Judy, one of the participants, reflected in her journal on an image she made during a mindfulness photo walk, describing qualities in her visual field that offered context to her experience as a human being. Attunement to these visual qualities gave rise to curiosity, as she was led to consider her own existence in relation to her neighbors.

> Light, color, shape, contrast. These are some of the ways I give context to my experience as a human being. Being human is a temporary condition. How do I touch others, the nameless ones who share this mailing wall with me? Do I even see that they exist beyond their numbered boxes? Who am I in relation to them? These thoughts lead me to wonder who will reach out first. (Photo 2.1)

Judy expanded on her experience as she described really being in touch with her experience at that moment. She recalled herself thinking of death as she noticed the contrasting colors in the room. Judy also described the moment she noticed the light from outside and the excitement that accompanied it.

> The mirror part of it made me think of how life is reflected back to us, but actually in this picture you don't see my face. You see the reflection of a glass door going to the outside world. When I look at it now, it looks cold, but it didn't feel cold when I took the picture. It felt like I was really in touch with being in that room.
>
> It partly caught my eye because of the color. Again, when I was sitting there, there's this gray area, and then there's this vibrant color, and then it's contrasting with the black of the mirror. It just made me think of death.
>
> When I took the picture, I thought, *Wow, there's something outside and it's light. Isn't that fantastic?*

As you begin to practice mindfulness and become more attuned, you will begin to feel a connection and resonance with your aesthetic environment. Landscapes and objects that you passively see every day might be seen and experienced anew. Making photographs from this place of deep

Photo 2.1. Judy, mailboxes. Photo courtesy of author.

resonance inspires a sense of curiosity and wonder that incites creativity and the meaning-making process.

CREATIVE EXPRESSION

Inseparable from personal and social fabrics dating back to ancient times, creative expression has been found in cave wall markings that depict efforts of survival, such as hunting and gathering. Creative artifacts in Indigenous cultures and modern civilizations have acted as tools to record and communicate how events and experiences took place, as well as serving as a powerful medium of psychosocial and spiritual expression that calls upon the eye, mind, and imagination.

Creative expression is engaged through a myriad of artistic modalities, including journal writing, music, poetry, drawing, painting, photography, dance, and sculpture. Photography can be understood as an expression of time and place, of experience, perception, and existence. All forms of creative expression are essentially means of communication, stretching beyond the egoic self, externalizing our thoughts and emotions, as well as uncovering unconscious processes and embodied memory.

Expressive writing can be used as a way in which people reflect on events and experiences and extract meaning from them. Journal keeping has been commonly used as a reflective practice to help individuals make sense of their experiences in the world. Expressive writing can be a creative yet gentle approach to accessing difficult emotions that otherwise might be kept inside. Journals are not just places for writing and recording images, since sketches, poems, and the use of color and form are among devices that can be used as vehicles to express ways of experiencing.

In addition to writing and journal keeping, personal photography is utilized as a creative modality that transcribes meaning, communicates feelings, and records memories of life experiences. Through photography, events that create significant memories in people's experiences and relationships may be honored as creative expression that celebrates life, love, and family from the artist's perspective. For example, scrapbooking can provide assurance of the meaningful existence of your family in the face of loss, and in a sense, it may facilitate a feeling of being protected when you are most vulnerable. Creative expression, such as journal writing and photography, has helped bereaved individuals begin to assess and accept loss.[5] Scrapbooking, for example, can be a tribute to and interpretation of life imbued with love. Both the creative process and a finished scrapbook can enable a bereaved person to not only accept the reality of death but also to validate life—and with that, the renewed possibility of healing and hope. Creative expression has the potential to bridge communication struggles that are often associated with verbal language during times of difficult life transitions.[6] Moving beyond verbal communication and integrating creative modalities can help us understand experiences in their fullness.

Mindfulness has been successfully integrated into art therapy and creative expression. Practicing mindfulness in creative expression can effectively invite conscious awareness in the present moment through mindful perception and concentration. While working with chronic adult psychiatric patients, art therapist Shaun McNiff discovered the helpful qualities that mindfulness can evoke through art expression.[7] Rather than ask patients what their art meant, McNiff encouraged them to contemplate the physical qualities of art objects by looking closely at them and describing their perceptions. This mindful approach on the act of looking

Photo 2.2. Janet, shadows. Photo courtesy of author.

was observed to foster greater awareness of patients' visual experience, exercising focused attention and increasing their ability to be both present and aware.

Creative expression is a means of communication and exploration that can reveal unconscious processes and embodied memories. Much as the camera captures light to illuminate objects, mindful photography can uncover what is inside us that is not so easily communicated. Janet, who participated in my study, described this aspect of the phenomenon quite beautifully.

> Those long shadows helped me realize that I feel infused by, bathed by light. I feel backlit: there's a light that shines through and illuminates, even reveals what's inside. (Photo 2.2)

Within and Without Mindful Photography participants engaged their experience more fully by moving beyond verbal communication to integrate the creative modalities of mindful photography and journal writing. They engaged in their experiences through mindful photography and then reflected on their images and created meaning from them. Creative expression through direct experience opened participants up to perceiving their experience with authenticity. Because creative expression emerges from the depths of our being, it has the power to release intense emotional pain by exploring and understanding our experiences. Making contact via photography can be a form of revelation as we confront the truth of life newly seen through photographs. People can open up to their experience as they become visually attuned through the lens of the camera, developing a sense of curiosity in relation to existence and their everyday phenomenal world.

Notes
1. Surya, 1997.
2. Rockwell and Valle, 2016.
3. Merleau-Ponty, Davis, and Baldwin, 2004.
4. Dufrenne, 1973.
5. Kohut, 2011.
6. Bijoux and Myers, 2006.
7. McNiff, 2011.

CHAPTER 3

Open Your Eyes. Open Your Heart.

In Chinese, the word for heart and mind is the same—Hsin. For when the heart is open, and the mind is clear they are of one substance, of one essence.

—STEPHEN LEVINE

DEATH AND DYING AND PHOTOGRAPHY ARE PARADOXICALLY CON-nected since photos present a way to visually suspend time and capture moments that are passing away. The magic that photography alludes to is its connection with present-moment awareness, which can, via the camera's very nature, bring the imagemaker into that awareness. In fact, simply holding a camera has the potential to induce a deep sense of awareness and groundedness. The process of making mindful images is akin to what Natoli and Suler described as therapeutic photography as "any self-initiated activity that is self-conducted and centered on pho-tography but includes no formal therapist."[1] Beyond being present in the moment and holding a camera, this way of photographing demands nothing from a person or the photographed object.

Photography can also be a spiritual practice that invites deep awareness and heightened consciousness into the reality in which those confronted by death are immersed. Photography is a tool for engaging the world with increased concentration through mindful awareness. By definition, mindfulness is understood as "open or receptive attention to and awareness of ongoing events and experience." Specifically embedded within photography is sustained attention to and awareness of what is occurring within the present moment.[2]

Openness and acceptance are key when we think about mindfulness as it relates to grief and loss and photography. You might notice throughout this book that the language associated with mindful photography is different than the typical language one might use while talking about, say, fine arts photography. I prefer to use the words, "I made a photograph or image," rather than "I took a photograph." Mindful photography is about cultivating an attitude of receiving rather than an aggressive stance of taking. The goal in mindful photography, and also in the grief process, is to open ourselves up to the process and accept what is offered to us in the moment. It is a practice of nonaggression and complete openness to the present. I recall a similar message in the book *True Perception: The Path of Dharma Art* by Chögyam Trungpa:

> Our message is simply one of appreciating the nature of things as they are and expressing it without any struggle of thoughts and fears. We give up aggression, both toward ourselves, that we have to make a special effort to impress people, and toward others, that we can put something over on them. Genuine art—dharma art—is simply the activity of nonaggression.[3]

Mindful photography and Buddhism are about what is in front of us and what we see with ordinary eyes. The story of the Buddha really took off when Siddhartha saw sickness, old age, and death but also grasped that these were the basic conditions of all beings. In one day, he went from ignorance of reality to knowledge to a commitment to change his life in accordance with what he realized. Buddhism, simply put, is founded on the acknowledgment of inconvenient truths. The practice of mindful photography is to make a choice, moment by moment, not to focus on how we want things to be, not to ignore the parts we wish weren't there, and not to close our eyes. It's seeing what's right in front of us, accepting that reality, and working with that reality. Mindful photography can help us choose to stay present with a reality that is difficult to see, and further, with the reflection inherent in the Within and Without Method, it can inspire us to create meaning from those experiences.

MINDFUL PHOTOGRAPHY

Awareness can be expanded through a variety of well-known spiritual practices, such as yoga, meditation, and even photography. Similar to yoga and meditation, photography is a readily available means of engaging the world with increased concentration and presence. It offers the possibility of a heightened consciousness for those who are willing to use it to deepen their understanding of the experience in which they are immersed. John Suler described mindful photography as such:

> In photography, mindfulness is like observing something for the first time, even though you may have looked at it a thousand times before. For example, when you've been away from home for a long period, and then, upon returning, you suddenly notice things to which you had become so accustomed that your eye failed to even register them any more—the decorations on the walls, the color of the rug, the view out the window. It's like that moment when you look at a family member or close friend and suddenly realize that you are truly SEEING them, as if for the first time, and not just looking numbly at them, as you usually do. Mindfulness is a deep kind of knowing.[4]

Suler mentions "a deep kind of knowing" that can emerge. This inner knowledge might also be understood as wisdom. When we are mindful, we open space within ourselves for wisdom to arise as we connect with our most precious internal resources. What follows are some examples of internal resources that can be challenging to access when we become overwhelmed by difficult life circumstances:

- The ability to connect and emotionally attune with our experiences
- The ability to shift perception and reflect on our own authentic experiences
- The ability to derive meaning from our own creations and experiences

- The ability to validate and self-soothe
- The ability to grow and transform through difficult experiences

Unlike conventional approaches to photography that so often emphasize the subject and object dichotomy, mindful photography sees beyond what is "looked" at. The focus is clear seeing and personal resonance. Photography, when practiced mindfully, can facilitate an aesthetic experience wherein one learns to temporarily overcome the subject-and-object dichotomy and disconnection. The process of mindful photography involves the acts of receiving, letting go, and learning to wait. You can let go of thinking, judging, self-evaluation, clinging, and rejecting, and accept whatever comes, good or bad.

In the process of mindful photography, psychological components surface as you become receptive to feelings and sensations, thus allowing your eyes to open more fully to the present moment. While resting in the present moment, you become both an observer and a participant, truly perceiving what is beyond appearances. Dufrenne described perceiving as an engagement that renders reflection and knowing.

> To perceive is not to register appearances passively—appearances which are meaningless in themselves. To perceive is to know—that is, to discover—a meaning within or beyond appearances which they offer only to the one who knows how to decipher them.[5]

When photography is practiced mindfully, it can be therapeutic and increase awareness and the capacity to create meaning through our experiences of grief. Meaning-making through grief is more fully explored in chapter 5. Essentially, those traversing the end of life are likely assisting someone in preparing to die or preparing for their own death. Those who can be mindfully present are more likely to experience emotional well-being and benefit from the transformative aspects of reflection on death, grief, loss, and meaning-making.

Mindful photography, as outlined in this book, elicits present-moment awareness through visual attunement. The practice can help mitigate the experience of anticipation of loss and the waves of grief in bereavement by helping you slow down mentally, thereby taking awareness away from the past or future and bringing it into the present moment. The participants' experience in this book revealed that mindful photography is a gentle way to nurture the mental space needed to open oneself to the experience of loss in the moment. The space that is created through the practice of mindful photography can prepare us to more fully explore our thoughts and emotions in relation to loss. Judy conveyed the experience of this open space as she reflected on her own practice of mindful photography: "Agreeing to take pictures made me more aware. It opened up a part of me."

PHOTOGRAPHY, DEATH, AND DYING

The invention of the camera changed the capacity to see the world, remember events, document time, and capture emotions. For nearly two centuries, photography has been used in a myriad of circumstances. Its main function of freezing time through the creation of a visual image reflects a desire to remember experiences, people, and things and to preserve them in a photograph. This desire may increase when the imagemaker is experiencing an impending loss or is in the grief process. Photography is a medium of communication that can be used to relate to others, inspire the meaning-making process, document events, and memorialize significant life events—even death.

In the nineteenth century, it was commonplace to take photos of the deceased and display them throughout parlors and bedroom walls. It is suspected that photographing dead loved ones was fueled by a desire to have and keep a visual remembrance of the person and event. Ruby, a visual anthropologist, believed that postmortem photography may have served some formal purpose in the mourning process.[6] Unfortunately, to what extent the process of taking photos of the deceased affected the mourning process remains unknown, as there is a lack of nineteenth-century literature related to mourning.

Postmortem photography was reinvented during the 1980s when hospitals began using photography with stillborn children and their families in neonatal units. In recent years, postmortem photography has grown in this same context with dying newborns. Todd Hochberg, a professional photographer who specializes in what he calls "Healing and Bereavement Photography," leads his own organization, Touching Souls. Hochberg's documentary-style photographs are made in hospitals for grieving parents in the short time they have with their dying or stillborn babies. These images serve as a gentle link to memories and feelings, offering an illustrated narrative that plays a significant role in helping parents to grieve and heal. As with any photograph, their meaning evolves and changes over time. Hochberg described his work in this way:

> While making meaningful photographs for grieving parents, I strive to be fully available, mindful for each moment and attentively supportive as their experience unfolds. As parents engage and soak up this emotional time, that very flow carries me along. Rooms often become very small as they fill with family, yet instead of feeling confined there exists for me, through intense human connection, an expansiveness and sense of oneness, of spirit.[7]

Roland Barthes described the relationship of death and photography in *Camera Lucida: Reflections on Photography*.[8] The subject of death was pivotal in Barthes's philosophy of photography, as he deemed the essence of that art form as "that has been." In fact, it was the death of Barthes's mother that most influenced his philosophy of photography and death, which emphasizes the passing of time and how a photograph represents existence—the notion of living and dying while at the same time acting as a still reference. Barthes's philosophy of death and photography is pertinent to the practice outlined in this book as it relates to our lived experiences of grief and reflections on dying, death, and loss.

How photographs bring to light the passing of time, death, and existential awareness was highlighted in my research involving caregivers who practiced mindful photography and reflection on their images. Caregivers described existential awareness in relation to their experiences of moments and the photographs' representations of moments that had passed. They experienced the temporal movement of contemplation as their consciousness oscillated between the reflective and the unreflective, the perceived and the lived. Through this process, the caregivers became increasingly aware of the movement of time and moments in time. The understanding of impermanence in relation to dying, death, and photography presented itself paradoxically as participants became aware of the impermanent nature of life through the making of still images and their reflection on them—documented moments in time. Judy described this aspect of the phenomenon quite succinctly as she reflected on the image she made of the Portland skyline.

> I think it represents everything that's always changing, and it's always moving, and I can capture, like in this photo. I can capture a moment in time. It looks like it's still, but it's not still. I can look at the skyline of Portland and see buildings that weren't there when I moved here. Now they're here. I'll be gone before they're gone. None of that seems very important. It just is. (Photo 3.1)

Photo 3.1. Judy, Portland. Photo courtesy of author.

As the participants continued the practice, they became increasingly aware of the passing of time and the all-pervasive impermanent nature of life and existence. Mindful photography helped them to slow down, focusing their attention outside of themselves on the aesthetic qualities of their experience. The combination of cultivating mindfulness through the lens of the camera—a tool that can figuratively freeze time—while anticipating the loss of someone they cared for, created a lived experience that inspired existential awareness through aesthetic perception.

The practice merged their inner experience of loss with their outer experience through aesthetic perception—the qualities of their environment. Emotional resonance occurred while they reflected on their images, employing the kind of depth that Dufrenne described in the realm of aesthetics as beyond everyday actuality.[9] That realm, he said, "is the necessary condition for values to be grasped, and for aesthetic values to be made accessible to the existential self." Existential awareness emerged as a repercussion of the ability to emotionally resonate with their images, perceive them aesthetically, and impart meaning to them that reached beyond the objects themselves. For example, Judy demonstrated this process as she connected her feelings of loneliness with the empty chair in the photograph she made. She recognized the image she made as a representation of the movement of time and the change that was occurring, both within herself and within her environment.

> I sit at the table where we used to enjoy long conversations over yummy food. I sit alone now. . . . I see the season changing; blossoms erupting from the ground, some potted, some not. I see the empty chair. I feel lonely; watching my thoughts as each day there is more work and less time for sharing. Spring is nearly here, but winter is in these four walls. It is a time of letting go, of being quiet, of jittery stillness. (Photo 3.2)

Some participants were moved to reflect on the eventuality of their own death, in addition to the loss of their family member or close friend. For example, Janet considered both her own death as well as her husband's as she reflected on the image she had made entitled "Looming Storm," connecting it with the anticipation of writing their obituaries.

Photo 3.2. Judy, table. Photo courtesy of author.

> It's not all storm, but it does feel to me as though there's this stuff looming. . . . Yes, there is this playfulness, and there is light, and there is joy in every day, but there's that other shoe that's going to drop. The medical power of attorney is all done and all of that, but the thing that we want to try and get done by the end of June is the obituary. I'm going to write them both . . . his and mine. (Photo 3.3)

Existential reflection on the impermanent nature of existence also surfaced as they became visually attuned to the movement of time that occurred as they witnessed their loved one's health decline and body lose functioning. For example, Carmen demonstrated this aspect of the phenomenon as she reflected on the image she had made of raindrops resting on a window screen. She associated the movement of the rolling fog with her dying mother-in-law's declining health, contemplating the reality that, like the raindrops, her mother-in-law would also disappear.

Photo 3.3. Janet, storm clouds. Photo courtesy of author.

Photo 3.4. Carmen, screen. Photo courtesy of author.

The fog will roll away quietly and leave a day with fresh starts. Not for everyone. . . . The rain makes me think of an emptiness in Ann's life. Just spots of her being left while the rest of her is silently rolling away like the fog. Sadly, we know the raindrops will disappear, as too will she. (Photo 3.4)

As participants reflected on their images, a conscious shift toward discovery was made. The intentional shift made way for a direct relationship between the world and self through reflection on the image created. Meaning began to emerge from that relationship. This process brings light to the wholeness of an experience as perception, thinking, and feeling become interconnected from the act of creating and reflecting on creations. As Janet reflected on some of her images, she described being more conscious of each moment that passed. Her attention was drawn to the image she made of the basket of petunias as she identified with the dropped petal. She observed the qualities in the image that represented her internal experience and feelings of loneliness and the inevitability of loss that happens in life. The process of noticing qualities in an image that reflects something inside of you is called *photographic equivalence*, which I discuss more fully in chapter 5. Through the practices focus on the lived experience of loss and meaning, creative expression through image making "answers a human need to portray in individual ways feelings and thoughts about what one is or, in certain cases, what one aspires to be; these feelings and thoughts being human experiences."[10]

I've not been preoccupied with wondering why ALS happened. Rather, I—and we—have been increasingly conscious of noticing each moment, of living what comes our way. Existence has felt more immediate.

There are, indeed, times when I feel cut off, even dropped. That basket of petunias made my breath catch in my throat. The single purple blossom on the pavers, fading by the minute, unsalvageable. That's life, I know. That flower a poignant, lonely reminder. (Photo 3.5)

DEVELOPING YOUR PRACTICE
Whether you are emotionally preparing for the death of a loved one or grieving the death of a loved one, the Within and Without Mindful

Photo 3.5. Janet, petunias. Photo courtesy of author.

Photography practice can position you to cultivate meaning and gain insights. You might also find that it relieves some fear, stress, depression, and angst that often accompany the grief process. Practicing mindful photography and reflecting on your images creates the space that is needed to process and integrate thoughts and feelings, revealing a much deeper sense of awareness, acceptance, and meaning. The practice might also awaken a renewed sense of curiosity and wonder!

The practice involves letting go of expectations, becoming attentive to moment-to-moment awareness, and accepting that which is present. In this process, psychological components surface as one becomes receptive to feelings and sensations, thus allowing the eyes to open more fully to the present moment.[11] As you begin to physically and mentally slow down, you begin to confront your grief and gain a greater comprehension of your relationship with loss and glean meaning from the experience. Perception, thinking, and feeling become interconnected within the act of making images. Meaning emerges as you reflect on your images and connect them with your inner experiences as represented by the objects photographed and the experience of mindful awareness. It is for this reason that I refer to this method as the Within and Without Mindful Photography Method. This concept is further explored in chapter 6 when I discuss photographic equivalent and symbolism, whereby your images might reflect your inner journey and consciousness.

This form of therapeutic photography utilizes two modes of expression through four steps that were inspired by a phenomenological art-based approach.[12] Each step builds on the other to mediate the experience of grief and increase awareness and deep reflection, thereby positioning you to cultivate meaning from your experience. As a therapeutic method, Within and Without is grounded in a process that brings light to the wholeness of your experience by utilizing both visual imagery and reflective journaling. Steps one to three below can be practiced as an independent practice. For the fourth and final step, a trained therapist or grief support group facilitator can facilitate a reflective dialogue about your photographs, thereby allowing deeper meaning and an expanded life narrative to emerge. This fourth step is more fully discussed in chapter 7 for those interested in integrating the method in therapy and grief support groups.

To begin, you will need a camera. A digital camera or your phone camera might work best because you can easily upload your images to your computer for the reflection step of the practice. Next, I recommend planning your mindfulness photo walks so that you will not feel rushed.

A photo walk might yield one image or five; there are no rules as to how many you make in one walk. Please consider leaving an ample gap of time between the time you make your images and the time you reflect on them in step three. For instance, you might schedule a mindful photo walk in the morning and, later that evening, reflect on your images for step three. Or you might schedule an evening photo walk and return to your images for step three the next morning. The gap of time is important because it allows you to return to your images with fresh eyes.

Last, I recommend that you plan step three in a location that is quiet and private so that you can truly be with your images and connect with them. And, again, plan a time that you will not feel rushed or pressured by time. Chapter 4 will show examples of those who explored their grief through this practice. You might notice that everyone's experience with the practice is a bit different. This is because grief is experienced and expressed uniquely; thus, the practice is not meant to be rigid, but rather, it is meant to be intuitive. As you review the steps that follow and proceed in your practice, I encourage you to understand this as a soft guide and not rules.

Step 1. Opening Up

Allow an opening in your day to engage freely through direct experience. You will practice becoming mindful and create images without directive or structured assignments—intuition and playfulness are encouraged.

Begin by sitting quietly through three deep breaths. Acknowledge your exhale as a letting go—prompting your body to relax and let go of any held tension. Notice where in your body you are clinging to or holding tension and try to soften those areas. When you feel more relaxed, slowly begin a mindfulness walk, with a gentle focus on your embodied experience (inner) and your visual experience (outer). In this step, you are practicing mindfulness and present-moment awareness through visual attunement—the experience of *noticing* and being drawn to something in your experience that causes you to slow down and be curious. Consider the reflection prompts below as you make images from a mindful space of non-judgment, curiosity, and wonder.

- Aware of your breath and the present moment, what in your visual field invites you to look closer and notice?

- Is there something that you see that inspires a moment of curiosity?

- Tune in to your aesthetic experience as you see color, texture, and shapes and as you hear various sounds and experience different smells.

Step 2. Making Contact

This second step is observed as a conscious shift toward creating. This step might be practiced a few hours after the first step or the next day. With your camera in hand, you will begin to engage in mindful photography with your experience of grief and loss in mind. I invite you to gently hold the awareness of your grief in mind as you connect with your environment.

Begin by sitting quietly through three deep breaths. Acknowledge your out-breath as a letting go—prompting your body to relax and let go of any held tension. Notice where in your body you are clinging to or holding tension and try to soften those areas. When you feel more relaxed, slowly begin a mindfulness walk, with a special focus on your embodied experience (inner) and your visual experience (outer).

Become visually attuned to the aesthetic qualities of your experience (color, shape, texture). Gently hold in your mind your lived experience of grief and loss. As you slow down and notice, let go of any judgment or expectations and allow a sense of connection to occur with your environment that invites you to pause, notice, and create, thereby making an image. Keep in mind that there are no guidelines as to how many images a photo walk might render, as it is unique to each photo walk. I encourage you to stay mindfully present and let your intuition guide you.

Step 3. Emotional Resonance

Step 3 invokes deep awareness through the act of reflection and intuiting. Allow several hours, at least, between steps 2 and 3, which will allow you to carefully look at and perceive your images in a fresh way, as if you are seeing them for the first time. You will spend time with your images without judging them, and journal about your experience of mindful photography without prematurely interpreting your images.

Begin by preparing your images for reflection, either by setting out prints or by uploading them to view on your computer screen. Next, prepare to write a journal entry either in a notebook or by typing on a document on your computer. With a focus on your emotional experience, carefully reflect on each image. Then, write a reflective journal entry about the moment you made the image and what struck you in that moment, inspiring you to slow down and pause, notice, and create. As you are looking at your images and preparing to journal, you might consider the following reflections.

- How did you feel in the moment you made the image?
- What invited you to pause, notice, and create?
- Looking at the image now, what stands out to you?
- Are there qualities about the image that mirror something inside of you?

Step 4. Authentic Insight

In the fourth and final step, a trained therapist or grief support facilitator intervenes to help expand your meaning-making process. This step integrates a process that Betensky calls "What-do-you-see?"[13] This question contains phenomenological aspects: individual perception, feeling, and seeing. The facilitator calls the question forth in a conscious effort, in Betensky's words, to "connect the artwork with the inner experience which was the prime mover in the artwork process that brought forth visual art expression."

In this step, you bring your images and journals to a session. You prepare your images either by presenting them in prints or on a computer. You and the facilitator reflect on your images one by one, allowing an explorative discussion to emerge about each image with a leading question: What do you see? After each image has been reflected on separately, you both look at the images as a whole with the questions that follow in mind.

- As you look at your images together as a whole, what do you see?
- Are there any themes that have emerged?
- Do your images relay a message for you?
- As reflected from your images, what might the title of your journey be?

The development of this practice was inspired by my personal experiences and my research study that explored the grief experiences of those who were caregiving for a dying loved one. Since that study, the method has been integrated to support other types of losses. In the subsequent chapter, we will review exemplars of those that have utilized the practice to explore their grief as it relates to anticipatory grief, bereavement, living with a life-threatening illness, and the lingering grief of a past loss. In chapters 5 through 7, we will explore how participants in my research study and those in chapter 4 experienced the practice as it relates to meaning-making, continuing bonds, and transformative growth.

NOTES

1. Natoli and Suler, 2011, p. 2.
2. Brown and Richard, 2004.
3. Trungpa, 2008.
4. Suler, 2013, p. 236.
5. Dufrenne, 1973, p. 335.
6. Ruby, 1995.
7. Hochberg, 2003, p. 6.
8. Barthes, 1981.
9. Dufrenne, 1973.
10. Betensky, 1995.
11. Zakia, 2013.
12. Betensky, 1995.
13. Ibid.

CHAPTER 4

Within and Without

The aim of art is to represent not the outward appearance of things, but their inward significance.

—ARISTOTLE

THE WITHIN AND WITHOUT MINDFUL PHOTOGRAPHY METHOD IS A way that you can explore your grief journey by slowing down and attuning with your environment. You might be drawn to notice qualities that reflect your inner process and aspects of your grief journey. Steps 1 and 2 of the method—opening up and making contact—can mediate difficult thoughts and feelings associated with grief because they bring you into present-moment awareness and inspire a shift toward curiosity. Furthermore, with reflection on the self-made images in steps 3 and 4— emotional resonance and authentic insight—the images gain personal and transformative significance. Serving as a mirror to your grief journey, your images act as a catalyst for meaning-making and even personal and transpersonal growth. Authentic insight surfaces as you create meaning based on direct experience and learn how to perceive your experience and trust yourself through the process.

This chapter illuminates the lived experience of grief explored through the Within and Without Method as applied to anticipatory grief, bereavement grief, and living with a life-threatening illness. The exemplars in this chapter consist of four participants, each representing a different kind of loss and processing their grief in different ways. While my original research in 2016 focused on those who were caregiving for a dying loved one, I have since integrated the method to help those experiencing other kinds of losses. The method can be used to cope, understand, and grow through any major life adjustment. For whenever we encounter a life transition, we are at the threshold of letting go of one thing and turning toward something anew. Some thresholds are more turbulent than others, and yet they always signify a grief process.

Like grief, each person's experience with practicing the Within and Without Method is unique to them, their relationships, and their own perceptions and personal expressions. The method is meant to be a gentle guide and an authentic expression; thus, it is not meant to be rigid or overly prescriptive. Although the participants in this chapter approached mindful photography in subtly different ways, as you will too, overarching themes emerged. These themes represent a shift in conscious awareness regarding the lived experience of grief and culminate to render a transformative grief experience: 1) visual attunement, 2) emotional resonance, 3) existential awareness, 4) inner strength, 5) gratitude, and 6) authentic insight.

MAGNIFICENCE AND INSIGNIFICANCE (ANTICIPATORY GRIEF)

Avery was anticipating the death of their mother-in-law, with whom they had a close relationship. They used the Within and Without Mindful Photography Method to process their anticipatory grief as they were approaching what would be a final goodbye. Avery chose to make their mindful photo walks outside, surrounded by wildlife. They noticed details in the natural world that mirrored aspects of their own grief journey. Connecting their inner experience with their outer experience, while in the natural world, inspired curiosity. The process also became a way for them to contemplate deeper questions surrounding life, death, and grief.

The theme of contrasts surfaced as they thought about the death experience of humans versus that of animals; they saw contrasting shapes and colors that gave rise to an awareness that there is both "magnificence and insignificance" and that things can be both "enormous and minuscule at the same time." As they reflected on their images in the fourth and final step, they said that a fitting title for their overall experience might be "Double Exposure," symbolizing "exposure of the natural physical world with my emotional process."

Step 2. Making Contact.

Photo 4.1. Avery, beach rocks. Photo courtesy of author.

Step 3. Emotional Resonance. It's not the prettiest view I came across today, but it is what washed up. Honor what washes up, into the sunlight.

Step 4. Authentic Insight. I was intrigued by the different shapes and the way things interacted just on the shore. And that tangle really spoke to the knots that I felt like I've had to untangle emotionally. There are pointy, sharp bits, and then there's smoother, happier memories that feel better underfoot, so to speak. The rocky angles to trip on that can be stumbling blocks along the path. And then there's a way to pick away through it. But there's no getting rid of any part of it. It's all part of the process.

There was a really nice variety, which really resonated with the variety of emotions and experiences that have come along with this process of preparing to lose somebody. And throughout the past few weeks, I've often been surprised at when I feel strong emotions, or don't seem to feel any emotions, or what just bubbles up to the surface from day to day. It sometimes feels out of context or a different shape than I might've expected. And so, just trying to take thoughts and feelings as they come, kind of like waves lapping up on a shore against the riverbank and just whatever comes up, is valid. And keeping that in mind and trying not to fight against it.

Step 2. Making Contact.

Photo 4.2. Avery, lichen. Photo courtesy of author.

Step 3. Emotional Resonance. What a striking, lovely life form, so easily passed by on the forest floor. Amazing individuals live and give and love and die daily. Stunning works of evolution fall from tree branches and wither among the leaves. Most of the time, most of us don't give it a second thought. The wonder and tragedy of it might crumble us if we did.

Step 4. Authentic Insight. That dualistic feeling of this one thing is so small and seemingly insignificant, just a little bit of lichen that fell off a tree, but at the same time, it is so complex and so lovely when you stop and think about it. And even just visually the contrast of the colors and shapes against the more dull brown background, it's both enormous and minuscule at the same time. And us humans are, too. Which is something that I've struggled with in that death is so common. Many deal with some kind of loss over the course of their lives. If we spent every day thinking about how incredible and yet how fragile and insignificant each life is, I wouldn't have energy for anything else. So, we can't really handle that degree of simultaneous magnificence and insignificance. And it has been mind-blowing to try to hold those two concepts at the same time. And this delightful little piece of natural artwork captured that for me.

Step 2. Making Contact.

Photo 4.3. Avery, path. Photo courtesy of author.

43

Step 3. Emotional Resonance. It's a long road of years to walk, and yet the sidewalk might end at any time. It's a long road of years to walk without a mother. It's a long road of years to carry loss. So many people keep on walking: some heavier, some lighter, almost nobody unburdened.

Step 4. Authentic Insight. It's a continuation of that concept of wrestling with just how common this process is and just the staggering weight that is so commonplace. All of us keep trudging down this sidewalk and it looks like a long way to carry that burden. At the same time, nothing's guaranteed, and it also highlights that. But we don't actually know how many years there are. So, we can't bank on there being a long road. There's both that uncertainty of where it's going and how long it is. And the certainty that each of us is carrying that there are prospective losses and struggles along the way.

Step 2. Making Contact.

Photo 4.4. Avery, ducks. Photo courtesy of author.

Step 3. Emotional Resonance. These ducks brought me some joy. Three pairs, waddling around and consulting with each other like they're deciding where to go for lunch. How does wildlife experience grief? Would it be better or worse to have "your person" just gone, without more understanding than that? I'm grateful for my consciousness and memories with loved ones, not to mention food and shelter. Even if emotional pain is part of it. It seems like a cold existence to be a duck.

Step 4. Authentic Insight. A lot of this process has felt like trying my emotions on within the surrounding environment and just seeing where they fit. And some of that has involved trying them on the surrounding wildlife. There's a lot of ducks and geese around and just wondering. They don't have medicine; they don't have clothes. They don't have the consciousness necessarily to understand death or anticipate it. And then trying the thought experiment on myself of, well, does that consciousness make this harder or less hard? And I think it makes it richer, both more painful and better. More wealth of good memories, more ability to treasure the time that we have in a way that a duck with a tumor would not understand. And so, it's a blessing and curse in that regard. But all in all, I'm not tempted to take up floating around on the river instead of sleeping in my own bed.

VEIL OF GRIEF (BEREAVEMENT GRIEF)

Josh accepted the invitation to practice the Within and Without Method to process the recent death of his grandmother. She was one of the most influential and important people in his life and exemplified unconditional love to him. When he began his first photo walk, however, it ignited feelings of grief for his father who died eleven years ago from multiple sclerosis (MS). He was moved to explore and process them both, honoring both relationships and the grief that lingered.

Reflections on the unknown aspects of death, such as the unanswered questions about an afterlife, were inspired by the night's fog and an air of mystery. Josh said that the fog was comforting because "it gave a tangible existence to existential feelings" that he was having in those moments. Contemplating the unknowns about death ignited a sense of excitement for Josh, because for him, the mystery was marked with a sense of wonder and possibility. These thoughts gave way to reflecting more about the special relationship he had with his grandmother. Josh's existential reflections acknowledged that death itself is individual: "no matter how many people are gathered at our bedside, if we are so lucky, we still experience death alone." However, upon further reflection, he was moved to consider an expanded view as he thought about the ways in which death connects us all and how we must all make that journey. Existential reflection was followed up with a deep sense of gratitude, love, hopefulness, and connection. "This existential confusion we have about why this is happening, and as we process through that, inadvertently, sometimes we get reconnected with the life that we have."

Step 2. Making Contact.

Photo 4.5. Josh, fog. Photo courtesy of author.

Step 3. Emotional Resonance. When beginning my mindful photography walk, I was surprised that I could feel how the recent loss of my grandmother ignited feelings of deeper grief for my father. The world around me was appropriately hidden by the night fog, and I found myself reflecting on the unknowns about death, where the consciousnesses of my loved ones are, and how the fog was a pretty good representation of the unknown regarding life after death. I took the first picture where only the lights of the street were visible. They reminded me of glimmers of hope that maybe one day, after death, I'll get to see my father again, hear him tell me he's proud of me, that he loves me, and maybe that he's sorry for the mistakes he made as a father. The darkness around the lights felt like a reminder of the unknown and unanswered questions I have about death and the pains of fear we often fear when facing the unknown.

Step 4. Authentic Insight. What I noticed was how the fog was really creating a barrier between me and the world around me. It made me think about how there is this veil between us and whatever comes next. It's completely unknown; we don't know what it is. So, I was reflecting on the unknowns about death, where we go, where my family is. It just really opened up the sense of the unknown.

It gave me the chills. Usually when we think of fog, there's a sense of unknown because it's often depicted in horror movies or in suspense and drama, or you'll see a fog roll in. There wasn't a fog rolling in, it just existed, and it felt stagnant in the space that I was in. So, it did create this air of mystery and unknown, but it wasn't frightening. I found it comforting. It felt like it gave a tangible existence to existential feelings that I have about death and about the afterlife if there is one. I reflected on the unknowns and where the consciousness of my loved ones were. You almost can't think of things like that and not have some sort of spiritual or, for some people, religious connotation attached to it. And I think that that's kind of what was giving me the chills was this notion that there's maybe possibly something greater than we're aware of and that our interconnectedness within existence is really present. Whatever this existence is, and meaning is, we have more connection to it than maybe we're aware of.

I kind of get excited about it all. It's like when I look at the photo and I think about how you can see that stuff is there. You can see that there's a car in the street and maybe some garbage cans, and you can see a light on the right side of the photo of maybe a front porch. You know that there are things there beyond it, but you don't know what they are. For some people, the unknown might be frightening. But for me, it feels exciting to think that maybe I'll get to see my dad again, or my grandma. It feels exciting that I get, to whatever degree that I do, another chance at consciousness and existence. And I don't know what that looks like or what that would be, but it's exciting for me. So, the fog is a veil between me and something possible.

Step 2. Making Contact.

Photo 4.6. Josh, light. Photo courtesy of author.

Step 3. Emotional Resonance. The second picture was taken when I saw the house at the end of the road more visible due to the Christmas lights still fitted around the home. It made me feel connected to my grandmother. As a child, she was always a light in the darkness that was my childhood. Regardless of the dark trauma and pain I was experiencing, she was always there to comfort me, tend my wounds, and remind me that love still existed in the world. I knew that no matter how much darkness I had to run through, she'd be there at the end of it. When she died of Covid, I was furious. It could have been prevented had the people around her gotten vaccinated, but instead, they let the darkness close in on her and take her life. The fog eventually gets us all. As my anger and grief subsided and I adjusted to a world without her, I began to feel the warmth of her love and saw the light she always shined at the end of that dark road. While we may share love for those we lose, ultimately, our grief is our own.

We experience it in ways no one else will. It changes us in ways it may not change other people. And when our time comes, no matter how many people are gathered at our bedside, if we are so lucky, we still experience death alone. The cold hand of finality embraces us, and we slip away, into the fog, while all the lives around us continue to go on, mostly unchanged. I stood in the street and thought about this for longer than anyone watching would have been comfortable with. And while it was heavy and sad and made me miss my father and grandmother even more, it also brought me comfort to know that every person, just like the two of them, will make that trip. If we are all doing it, it can't be that scary. And then the heaviness of the fog and night lifted, and I felt more grateful for their love, their lessons, and hopeful that I'll get to see them again.

Step 4. Authentic Insight. I took this after thinking of my father, and there was some sadness. I couldn't really see much around me. And then when I turned down the street, it was like the fog lifted just enough, in part probably due to the lights at the end of the street, but it felt like there was an answer being shown to me. And it just kind of hit me that, prior to this place now, the only place I ever considered home was my grandparents' house. The Christmas lights on the house at the end of the street made me think about how big Grandma would do Christmas. The answer that I felt like I was getting was maybe to a question that I didn't even know I had, and that was where do I connect myself to love? I experienced a great deal of abuse and trauma growing up, and it's always been a question with myself, and then people who I've spoken to about it would ask, "How did you grow up to be kind and compassionate when you weren't shown much of that at all?" And that night it was like, "Well, Grandma." I always felt safe with her.

I don't think I was really aware of it until recently just how much of a strength and kind of a teacher she was on what it means to be loved. When I came out as gay, she'd just listen to stories about whomever I was dating, and she never had any judgment. It was just the space of unconditional acceptance and love. And I think that the photo specifically was telling me that even with the unknowns of death, even with the disconnect that we often feel when someone dies, that there is still that thread that keeps us connected and together, that through the veil of the unknown, I still have a connection to her, and that connection was the love that she provided me, the love that I still feel.

So, seeing this lit up home with Christmas lights at the end of the road, I just thought a family lives there, and they celebrated Christmas, and they've had dinners together, and they've had all these good and bad experiences that families have, and it's home for them. And that's what Grandma's house is, for me.

Step 2. Making Contact.

Photo 4.7. Josh, field. Photo courtesy of author.

Step 3. Emotional Resonance. I hadn't intended on being mindful of my grief and the lives of my father and grandmother but found myself thinking intently and fondly of them. I was grateful I got to be with my father when he died and was able to spend my grandmother's last birthday with her before she also died. So, I snapped a pic of a green field, large barn in the background, under an overcast sky. It felt like life, and it made me feel grateful for my partner and our dogs and the life I have.

Step 4. Authentic Insight. I remember being grateful and feeling like this whole cycle that we go through, with life and death, birth and growing up . . . it was a rainy day, it was like this rejuvenation . . . and, these things have to happen. We have to have rain to have new growth, and we have to rely on the earth for sustenance and, to a certain degree, shelter. I mean, that's how we get bricks and wood for building houses. So, there was this sense of interconnectedness with the world around me, and it was tied directly with *I am who I am because, be it good or bad, the experiences that I had growing up.* I am who I am because of a lot of bad experiences that I had with my father, or the things he was involved with, and the good that came from my grandmother. So, while not everything is positive, there is a way for us to process the things that we've been through and achieve a sense of gratitude for having had them. It doesn't necessarily mean that we would want it or that we would wish it on another person. I have been able to make meaning out of the experiences that I've had, and I'm grateful for that.

This one stood out, because mostly what you see is the sky, the gray, cloudy sky, and the unknown of what's beyond that. But then there's still this large portion that's connected to where I'm standing. And then, in the background is the barn, which, for me at the time, was representative of my past and my family and growing up on a farm in Kansas. So, it was just this connection between the three.

What it reaffirmed for me was life. Grief, it turns everything upside down; my own experience is that it can make things not make sense. This existential confusion we have about why this is happening, and as we process through that, inadvertently, sometimes we get reconnected with the life that we have.

Feeling Cared For (Grief with Life-Threatening Illness)

Ruth has lived with a life-threatening illness of kidney failure, among other health challenges that further complicate her diagnosis and well-being. How she feels day to day can vary a great deal, making it hard to get outside. She said it's "been a heck of journey with my illnesses as to where I am emotionally, physically, and spiritually. It's not been easy." Grief surfaced for Ruth not only as her life was threatened by major illnesses but also as she traversed many limitations in daily life. She also described how she became a grandmother and missed out on traveling to see her children and grandchildren and "all that idealistic stuff" that didn't happen for her. The grief experienced with major illness can be multi-layered and include fear of death, loss of functioning, and loss of a future plan and vision.

Ruth described the way in which physical pain can make it hard to embrace positive things in her life. Her images and journal entries, she said, reflected the spiritual journey she was on in being more present, being instead of doing, and "instead of waiting for something pleasant to happen, I am looking for it, trying to notice." Her last image of roses was symbolic for her in many ways and carried with it a message of connection. She was moved to recollect a difficult life stage and how at that time she learned that she could offer herself kindness by getting herself flowers. Roses specifically reminded her of her mother, and they also reminded her that she was indeed cared for.

> I think it's telling me that I'm not totally uncared for or unloved, because sometimes that's what it feels like when I'm working so hard and taking care of everything. I'm associating feeling cared for because it's pleasant and it's not hurting me. I feel cared for instead of feeling hurt. It's pleasant, not unpleasant.

Step 2. Making Contact.

Photo 4.8. Ruth, windsock. Photo courtesy of author.

Step 3. Emotional Resonance. I woke to a gray-sky morning for about the tenth day in a row. Earlier than my norm due to poor sleep. I was able to sit on my back deck because the winds had decreased to gentle breezes. The windsock was barely moving, and nature sounds were gentle. In what seemed like seconds but was actually minutes, the gray sky broke up, [and then] white clouds, blue sky, and sunshine appeared. I felt myself take a deep breath, and a smile formed.

Step 4. Authentic Insight. This shows all the years I live for and that I am learning to look for something positive to hang on to. That day, the breeze was comfortable. Then the light was so obvious, because to the left of this image, there were still dark clouds. It felt positive. And I smiled, hoping it would last awhile.

Step 2. Making Contact.

Photo 4.9. Ruth, greenery. Photo courtesy of author.

Step 3. Emotional Resonance. I very often attend mid-week services at my Episcopal church that includes optional healing prayers at the altar. My morning did not go as planned. I decided I would visit the chapel in private. Instead, I found myself outdoors in an adjoining little alcove for my first time. Sitting on the bench, I listened. It was quiet.

I felt hugged by the Greenery of God's creation because it nearly surrounded me.

Step 4. Authentic Insight. The chapel was open; I could have gone
in there. But I think because we've had such gray and rainy weather, I
took advantage of the nice day. And also, I live a very isolated life; I'm
indoors 90 percent of the time. We moved when Covid happened, so
that interfered with making friends, plus my health kept putting me in
the hospital. It's been hard to be isolated and indoors.

For four months, I haven't been outdoors because of the heat. I
took advantage of that day, and instead of going indoors to meditate,
pray, or just be quiet, I said, "Oh, let me sit out here." I knew this existed
but hadn't done it. It was fine because it's God's creation to me. The
greenery showed the [arched window of the] church, so I was being
churched anyway. It was kind of a treat. I wasn't hearing any traffic;
there was none of the business or noise. It was peaceful.

Step 2. Making Contact.

Photo 4.10. Ruth, slippers. Photo courtesy of author.

Step 3. Emotional Resonance. Elevating and resting (while trying to hold on to humor) my feet as I recover from painful swelling and gout to my left foot. Just a touch envious of Snoopy being able to fly.

Step 4. Authentic Insight. That foot really hurt, and I was frustrated. But yet, I live in a place, a physical environment, that people love, but I've been so preoccupied with survival that I can't embrace the luckiness of being in such a beautiful new home on the water. When you're in pain, emotional or physical, you don't embrace that. It's hard for me anyway. I can't go to church again because I'm in pain, and I had to put this foot up. So, I put these slippers on, and when I propped them up, I could see those images. . . . I see them all the time; they're cute. But this time, I'm looking at it, and I go, "Oh boy, I wish I could fly. If I were flying, my foot wouldn't hurt when I walked." Trying to laugh, trying to keep it light. I'm working really hard at it, though.

Step 2. Making Contact.

Photo 4.11. Ruth, roses. Photo courtesy of author.

Step 3. Emotional Resonance. I love flowers and enjoy flower arranging. Taking a walk on a cool, sunny, breezy fall day, I was pleasantly surprised to see a few late bloomer roses. I held them and sat on the cement bench for an unknown amount of time feeling happy.

Step 4. Authentic Insight. Those roses made me happy. They were late bloomers, so they caught my attention right away because everything's starting to dry up. The grass next to our home here is turning brown. So, to see this bright-red, perky color really caught my eye. I decided to trim them and make an image. Around my divorce time, when I was in my early thirties and my children were only five and eight years old, there was so much pain. But I realized that I could treat myself well. And so, I treat myself with flowers. Especially when I feel there's been a stretch of just drudgery, I'll purposely go out and get flowers. But these I did not purposely go out for; they were a surprise.

Roses hit me in a lot of different ways because my mother loved roses, and sometimes, that was a nickname for me: Rosa. I even have a little ceramic rose that belonged to her. So, I had a lot of messages come into my brain when I saw them. Messages of connection. There's been very little softness and love and kindness toward me or protection. It doesn't happen that often, so I definitely notice it when it does happen. I think it's telling me that I'm not totally uncared for or unloved, because sometimes, that's what it feels like when I'm working so hard and taking care of everything. I'm associating feeling cared for because it's pleasant and it's not hurting me. I feel cared for instead of feeling hurt. It's pleasant, not unpleasant.

I'm on a spiritual journey with working on being present and being still and just being instead of doing. This is probably reflecting that journey. I move toward acceptance, dealing with my reality. And, instead of waiting for something pleasant to happen, I am looking for it. I can notice the light moments. However heavy things are, the light will soften things and lighten the load. The pain can be softened, and even the fear can be softened. Sitting down and writing about the photos, that helped me really be aware. For me, it made the moment that caught my eye or caught my heart enjoyable for a longer time.

MIND AND SPIRIT FREE AT LAST (LINGERING GRIEF)

Gracie James was moved to reflect on the past loss of their father that occurred twenty years earlier. Their father became sick with a debilitating illness while Gracie James was still relatively young. They recall their father being a vibrant, robust, physically abled Italian guy, to nearly dying with a brainstem encephalitis, and then confined to a wheelchair and losing all of his motor capabilities and speech. Gracie James chose to visit a close-by field where their father taught high school and where part of his ashes was spread. The high school building is no longer there, but Gracie James still feels a connection to that space and walks there, to the now open field, to have conversations with him. As they walked through the space for this project, they also walked through time, revisiting memories of their father and lingering pieces of grief. The inner landscape of emotions, thoughts, beliefs, and hopes from the past are stirred, followed by a widening space to hold the ever-evolving relationship with their father.

Step 2. Making Contact.

Photo 4.12. Gracie James, gate. Photo courtesy of author.

Step 3: Emotional Resonance. Entering the gate. Permission to feel grief, the safety to ask questions, and share stories of shame. Taking risks to notice how we are inhabiting space, wrestling with anger and self-blame, a little less alone.

Step 4. Authentic Insight. I was literally entering into that space a little less alone as I was being led by this project. Invited in to create a space to hold what's here but has no containment other than my own internal world. So, the container is this project and these photographs. I think that these pictures made it so that the internal experience corresponded to something to make sense of the experience.

That used to be a parking lot, where I learned to drive. That gate is the only thing that remains of the school. I have this very strong memory of seeing my dad at work and being in that building. Going into the space, for me at the time, was going where the "big people" are. Now, there are paths that weave through where people have worn down by walking different routes with their dogs or with themselves. It's really a great place to practice walking meditation without all the bells and whistles. Just walk.

Step 2. Making Contact.

Photo 4.13. Gracie James, field. Photo courtesy of author.

Step 3: Emotional Resonance. It's the morning. I walk into the field where I once went to school and where I learned to drive a car, where my dad once taught high school. The building was torn down because of mold and radon, and later, this was where my sister spread some of my father's ashes. Although I anticipated coming here, I didn't anticipate the space looking as empty as it rest, even though my mind knows there hasn't been a building here for more than a decade. There's no longer a building just like there's no longer my dad's body here. And there's an excitement and longing for there to be a presence, a physical presence that is different than the physical reality that is laid out before me. Because I want others to see, I want others to see. I want others to see my losses, my father's body, the school that was once here. As if these objects would be able to convey or communicate a shared meaning.

Step 4. Authentic Insight. I really laid it out there, didn't I! I remember feeling that there are so many competing stories, especially when someone is gone. There are the stories that the living tell about the person, and then there are the different memories that come up, or the wishes for there to have been something different. I was moving through those ghosts, or words, or stories. And by acknowledging them, it was like, "I am here. I'm still here in this forum, and I know that all of this other stuff is here, including this person who created me."

But there was something less haunting about being in that space. I think especially what I'm talking about is how my grief shows up as anger initially. My first knee-jerk [reaction] is to be pissed about things that are taken. But there is something more than anger. The anger can be there, but it doesn't stop time, it doesn't stop pain, it doesn't stop anything. It's just a piece of the puzzle. And there's an excitement and longing for there to be a presence, a physical presence, but it's different than the physical reality that's laid out before me. I'm not manifesting this man, his presence. I'm allowing the meaning of this relationship, my ideas about the meaning of this person, to be complicated, to be more than just a dyad. It's like there's a whole generational lineage going on with me, with the trees, with this. . . . You wouldn't know there was a parking lot under all that grass. So, I guess it's just all the layers.

How can you ask others to know your grief? I want to feel felt in this. To invite someone into something that's sorrowful is a challenge because people tend to get overwhelmed really quickly or not know how to handle it. But also, it's a thing of, "Do you want to know my father? Do you want to know these buildings I passed through? That's to know me, do you want to know these things?"

Definitely, as we're talking about this, a lot is being stirred. So, it's not actually that far away, which is incredible, right? And yet, so much time has passed, and there's distance. We're looking into this distance, and there's depth. This process was for me about building some distance or space. There's the difference between being overwhelmed by grief and being able to be with grief, alongside grief. So, instead of me being grief-stricken or devastated by some relational loss, this is building the space. I'm walking with you. I'm walking alongside you.

Step 2. Making Contact.

Photo 4.14. Gracie James, path. Photo courtesy of author.

Step 3: Emotional Resonance. Loss and grief is a shared meaning, but we all make distinct things out of it. I remember my dad bringing me here. Holding his hand. Walking down the hallway. As I walk this trail now in the grass, I go in the same direction as the cigarette machines and teacher's lounge. My body is holding onto the full sense memory of 1978, and I am breathing in 2018. We are a part of something larger. You and I are light and dirt.

At first, when my sister spread his ashes here, I was angry because I thought, *How can you put his ashes where dogs take a shit?* I had put my chunk of ashes in the ocean and had imagined that his spirit would be able to flow between Oregon and Hawaii, back and forth between two places that he loved. I attached meaning that was meaningful to me, and I attached a judgement to what was meaningful to my sister and now here I am only three blocks away from where I live, and I appreciate it because her act brought attention to this relationship to this inner and relational landscape over time. The environment does not reflect who my father is. The environment has changed. At some point, there will be something else built here. For now, it is empty. A field of weeds where his ashes were spread.

My feelings shift. The loss is something that is known in the cells, its feeling ever-changing, now known as a wave to ride. When you stare into the ocean, you learn to distinguish all layers of color and light as you give in to seeing in a new way of shape and movement.

Step 4. Authentic Insight. I just thought of him, if he heard this, being a man of few words after his illness, he probably would've been like, "Good." As in, I'll accept that. I have so few memories of my dad bringing me many places. He wasn't the most active parent and had mental health issues and other things going on. But one of the things that I always remember is trying to catch up with him, him just being this languid corduroy guy and trying to catch up with him, and then, he would take me with him. Now, I'm catching up with him, but he's everywhere, and he's not going to take me somewhere of his choosing. I'll be a part of that decision-making. I think what I want to say, and this came up with the last one, are the things that didn't happen. I really wanted my dad to get me out of Dodge. I wanted my dad to take me somewhere else. And once he became seriously disabled, I knew that was not going to happen. I knew that he was not going to be the hero that was going to take me out of something that I really needed help getting out of. I think that's the thing that was stuck in 1978 and 1982, the wish for more. And it was cut off by illness, it was cut off by death, that wish. And so, it's a journey. We're journeying along. I'm remembering I felt lonely in that. Like, "Where's my partner? Where's a friend? Where's my family?"

The loneliness surfaced as I was moving. It's interesting to look back now at that gate and think that there's something blocking me. When I first started the walk, there was a lot of anxiety. I think in moving and in choosing images and in relating to the space got me out of that stuckness of anxiety. And then, what was that covering up? Just a deep, deep, deep, deep longing, and that kind of loneliness of "this is mine."

Right before he passed, we had a head-to-head where I wanted acknowledgment of all of these things. And I was like, "What about me?" And he looked at me, and he was like, "What about me?" Now, I'm like "Okay, it's not you or me, that's trauma talking." Now there is more healing. And that's the sense of time, too. I'm fifty-three now, so I have less need to lean on my ego, so I can relate more to him. And I think if he'd been able to live longer and it'd been less painful for him to be here, I think he would've been able to get there, too. I actually have a better relationship with my dad now than when he was living, hands down. I feel his support more now.

I'm not a religious person, and I'm not particularly spiritual either. And I don't think that I've made things up; I mean, I know people say that they get tired of one-way conversations with the dead and really want to hear something. I do hear him, and I don't think it's my fantasy world. I think that I'm hearing an energy thread that has a depth, that has a distance to it, and there's points along the line where we can meet. Maybe that's why there's all these trails, literally walking to walk it out, to walk out the frustration, the anger, the sorrow. But also, because I don't know how long this line is. I don't know; I like to think it's long.

I love that there's this field of weeds. I find emptiness very soothing. I did commercial fishing for a season. And looking into the depths of the water and looking for movement was a trip on the eyes because you think like, "Oh, it's just sort of a blue-green thing going on in there." But then you're like, "Oh, wow, there's so many layers if I look enough." And this was a beautiful thing to be like, "Yeah, there's a lot of layers. I'm not just sad and mad. There's a lot more going on."

My dad's mother visited me last week in a dream. I woke up thinking about her and this thing about cellular memory and how she held it together, held the family in a true matriarch style. And I thought, "Oh, I can do this. My grandma was tough. I don't have to fix anything. I have to take care. I have to take care. There's ways I want things to go, but I don't know if that's how they'll go, but I need to take care along the way, moment by moment by moment." And I think that that's something that I didn't come up with, I think that's in my cells, and is good to acknowledge.

Step 2. Making Contact.

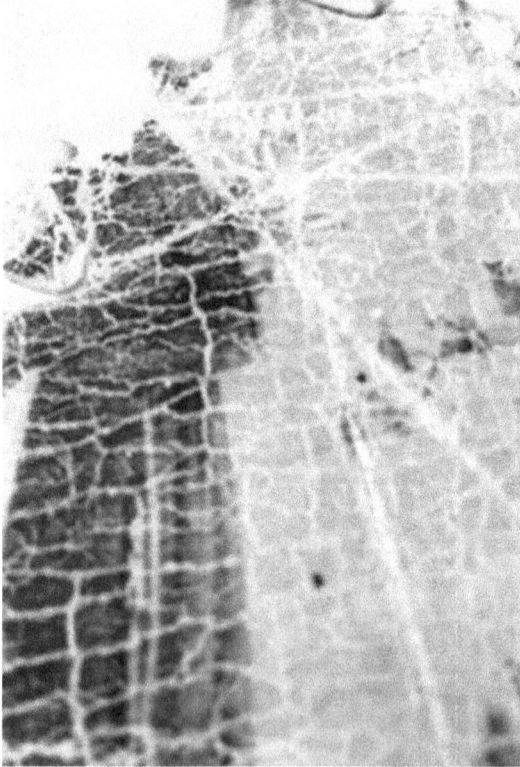

Photo 4.15. Gracie James, prayer card 1. Photo courtesy of author.

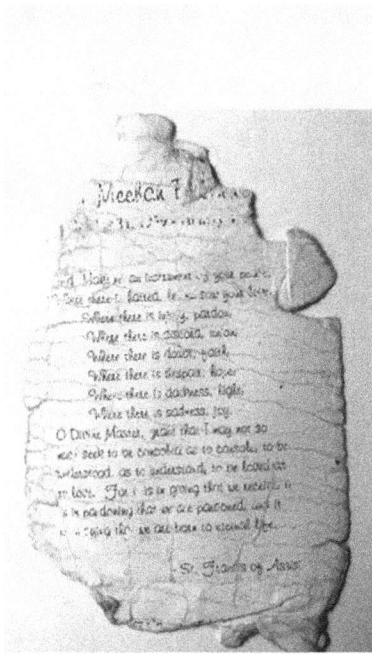

Photo 4.16. Gracie James, prayer card 2. Photo courtesy of author.

Step 3: Emotional Resonance. In my wallet your prayer card is tattered, yet in our conversations, you are getting younger over time. Forever at my birth. When you left this plane, the wind swirled a storm, and it really did howl. In the early morning of January 4, 2008, I saw you in the bed and your body looked peaceful because for the first time in twenty-eight years none of your muscles were twisted up in pain, and you are now six feet tall to remember.

Step 4. Authentic Insight. I just got some shivers listening to you read that entry back to me. Isn't it amazing what words can do; they can bring us right back to a place that would be easy to not remember? My partner said when [my father] died, "I bet he can walk now." And I think that that was part of the wish. My mom always talked about, "Yeah, when I met your dad, he was that guy who would just grab the tree and turn himself sideways and go upside down and flip around." And so, he was a very physical person who messed around

65

with space and having a body. And I really felt like his body trapped him here in a way that didn't align with his mind. And so, I was really hoping and felt that without his body, his mind and spirit could move freely.

CHAPTER 5

Choosing Light

The wound is the place where the Light enters you.

—RUMI

IN THIS BOOK, THE TERM "CHOOSING LIGHT" REFERS TO THE ABILITY TO acknowledge grief by choosing to look at it rather than staying in the dark and avoiding it. It is the willingness to embrace all aspects of ourselves, including the difficult emotions that so often accompany loss. By opening up, we can face our grief and explore our experiences more fully. I am reminded of a quote by the famous poet Robert Frost: "The best way out is through." The combination of mindfulness and creative expression, engaged through the camera, becomes a gentle guide *through* grief. However, more than *getting through* is the recognition that one is changed and strengthened from having gone through such a journey. When you choose the path of seeing and being with your grief, you mingle with the most authentic parts of yourself and you can realize your creative potential. When the darkness we feel from grief makes contact with light, there can be a sense of wholeness that washes over, and we realize that there is so much more to learn and so many more ways to grow in this lifetime.

MEANING-MAKING

Meaning-making generally involves the reflective process of stepping back from an experience to connect it with a deeper understanding and more expansive view. In stepping back, you create the space to marvel at a larger life narrative that unfolds in relation to the past, present, and future. Gracie James described in chapter 4 a sense of distance and depth and that being indicative to them building a space for their grief.

> We're looking into the distance, and there's depth. This process was for me about building some distance or space. There's the difference between being overwhelmed by grief and being able to be with grief, alongside grief. So, instead of me being grief-stricken or devastated by some relational loss, this is building the space.

Because the death of a loved one disrupts previously established interests, goals, and expectations linked to relationships, it poses a significant challenge to existing meaning structures and one's sense of identity.[1] Our loved ones often serve as anchors and reference points for who we are. When that reference point is gone, you might feel ungrounded, as if the rug has been pulled out from underneath you. Suddenly, you don't know who you are anymore! Although it is hard to see in the moment, these experiences are often the prelude to discovering your most compelling ability and precious inner resource—your ability to create meaning from your experiences.

Personal growth takes place as one addresses the challenges of losing a loved one, accepts the loss or impending loss, and begins to make sense and create meaning through the process. It is said that to experience personal growth, one must enter and engage the "reconstruction" process; that is, for growth to occur, one must process and reconcile the meaning of the loss of one's life or "make sense of it."[2] Sense-making asks "Why?" and "Why me?"; benefit-finding asks, "What have I gained?"; and life significance asks, "What now?" and "What matters?"[3] These differences are important because they help us assess where we might be in the reconstruction process. Ultimately, it is through the process of reconstructing that you come to see yourself in relation to others in a different light, reevaluate priorities, and appreciate life in a new way.

Meaning reconstruction evolves as a process whereby "grieving is the attempt to reaffirm or reconstruct a world of meaning that has been challenged by loss."[4] In a more recent study, photography was used to explore whether using photographs as the basis for a grief narrative would be associated with the meaning-making process while in bereavement.[5] As one might imagine, the combination of words and images allowed for greater nuance, meaning, and insight for participants to better understand their lived realities of grief, thus inspiring a reconstruction process. This study validates the idea that images can and often do serve as points of reference for creating meaning through the grief process.

Related to bereavement but that which happens before a loss is anticipatory grief. A number of studies indicate that meaning-making is the most transformative mediator for those who are caregiving and anticipating the death of their loved one.[6] In fact, it was the most important aspect among caregivers' perceived gains. In addition, awareness, acceptance, and meaning-making are key contributors to a positive death experience as well as to a shift in existential and spiritual perceptions.[7] This suggests that increased self-awareness in relation to an impending loss of a loved one supports preparation for the loss, positioning one to cultivate meaning, gain insight, and move toward accepting the loss. As you anticipate a close death, mental and emotional preparation for that loss can take place through the meaning-making process and influence a shift toward letting go and accepting the loss.

Practicing the Within and Without Method can help emotionally and psychologically prepare you for a loved one's death because it helps you stay present and aware of your emotions and thoughts as the death is happening. After a loss, the practice can support movement toward reconstruction as it ushers you forward through your grief journey. The increased awareness can position you to create meaning from your experiences as you reflect and emotionally resonate with the images you made, thus engaging the reconstruction process. The reflective space created for the meaning-making process can provide existential and spiritual nourishment as you confront a loss and come to a greater comprehension of your relationship with the dying person or your own death and with death in general.

Although a struggle at times, seeking meaning through grief is a human's way of making sense of a loss. We attempt to preserve a sense of continuity with who we have been while also integrating the reality of our changed world and life narrative. Meaning-making processes can help you stay connected to yourself and others as you adjust to a new reality. Because meaning-making involves connection and receptivity, it offers a unique opportunity to connect with the more caring and loving aspects of ourselves, which Freeman described as "our own potential goodness coming into being in tandem with the reality of the Other."[8] The practice outlined in this book acts as a framework and scaffolding to assist with meaning-making whereby one can feel a sense of agency and connection through their grief journey. In chapter 4, Gracie James compared the process to that of a holding space and container for the meaning-making process.

> I was being led by this project. Invited in to create a space to hold what's here but has no containment other than my own internal world. So, the container is this project and these photographs. I think that these pictures made it so that the internal experience corresponded to something to make sense of the experience.

SYMBOLISM

The word "symbol" comes from the Greek term for throwing together, bringing together, integrating. The process of symbol formation can be understood as a continuous process of bringing together and integrating the internal with the external, the subject with the object, and the earlier experiences with the later ones. Creating symbols in context to your grief experience presents a way of integrating the lost relationship into your life. Hanna Segal, a British psychoanalyst whose work in the 1950s focused on a psychological approach to aesthetics, understood symbol formation as a creative activity directly linked with the mourning process. She suggested that healthy mourning might be supported by a restorative process of symbolic transformation in which the lost relationship returns as a living symbolic presence.[9]

> Every situation that has to be given up in the process of growing, gives rise to symbol formation. In this view symbol formation is the outcome of a loss, it is a creative act involving the pain and the whole work of mourning.[10]

Creating symbols through grief can carry us forward through a mourning process where our internal feelings of grief become outwardly expressed, thus inspiring meaning-making and ritual processes. (This idea is more fully explored in chapters 6 and 7, where I discuss continuing bonds and rituals.) The difference between grief and mourning is the internal versus external nature of the processes. While grief relates to the thoughts and feelings that accompany a loss, from sadness to anger and longing, mourning is how feelings of grief are externalized.[11] Grief is an experience that is often difficult to put into words. Moving beyond verbal communication and into integrating creative modalities can be helpful and sometimes transformative. Symbol formation is a creative act that can help you express your grief, and at the same time, it can be a *way of knowing* that helps you understand your experience more fully.

In chapter 4, Josh reflected on the image he made of a streetlight glowing on a dark, foggy night. The fog in the photograph symbolized for him all the unknowns that surround death and the unanswered questions about the afterlife, while the glowing light symbolized glimmers of hope.

> The world around me was appropriately hidden by the night fog, and I found myself reflecting on the unknowns about death, where the consciousnesses of my loved ones are, and how the fog was a pretty good representation of the unknown regarding life after death. I took the first picture where only the lights of the street are visible. They reminded me of glimmers of hope that maybe one day, after death, I'll get to see my father again, hear him tell me he's proud of me, that he loves me, and maybe that he's sorry for the mistakes he made as a father. The darkness around the lights felt like a reminder of the unknown and unanswered questions I have about death and the pains of fear we often feel when facing the unknown. (Photo 4.5, page 46)

In the interview for Step 4, Josh further reflected on the details of the image and their impact on him in those moments. He discussed how fog is often used in movies as a way to evoke suspense, and how although he was not frightened, there was an air of mystery. The experience of fog in those moments, paired with the symbolic nature of fog, was validating in that it offered a "tangible existence to existential feelings" and thoughts that he was having.

> It made me think about how there is this veil between us and whatever comes next. It's completely unknown; we don't know what it is. So, I was reflecting on the unknowns about death, where we go, where my family is. It just really opened up the sense of the unknown.
>
> It gave me the chills. Usually when we think of fog, there's a sense of unknown because it's often depicted in horror movies or in suspense and drama, or you'll see a fog roll in. There wasn't a fog rolling in; it just existed, and it felt stagnant in the space that I was in. So, it did create this air of mystery and unknown, but it wasn't frightening. I found it comforting. It felt like it gave a tangible existence to existential feelings that I have about death and about the afterlife, if there is one.

Chögyam Trungpa Rinpoche described symbolism as "a question of gaining new sight. It is being extremely inquisitive to see things in their own nature, not always wanting to change things."[12] An inquisitive mind is indeed an open mind that is receptive and thus able to work through the experience of grief and mourning. Perhaps a central task of mourning is to make sense of the tension between the absence of our loved one and the continuing presence of an emotional relationship with them. It is here that Carl Jung's notion of a transcendent function might be an important element of the mourning process because it enables conflicting opposites to be transcended via an emergent symbolic realization.[13] Jung believed that the unconscious often breaks through to help us through life adjustments, whereby a transcendent function takes place.[14] The function of symbol formation might very well be a self-intervention that can transform grief and everyday experiences, awakening us to new insights. You might also think about symbol formation as part of the reconstruction process of grief, when your mind is ready to ask the questions of benefit-finding and life significance: "What have I gained?," "What now?," and "What matters?"

If you can slow down and spend time looking at things and being with things directly, clarity and insight might coalesce through symbolism. Particularly while in grief, there can be a sense of wholeness that occurs to offer comfort and restoration. In this way, the images you make and the meaning you create from them can serve as transitional objects of grief, providing a sense of security and symbolic connection to your deceased loved one. Your level of openness and receptivity through grief is vital to experiencing the restorative and meaningful impact of creating symbols as part of a larger life narrative and meaning-making process. Because so much of our lived experience is veiled and hidden behind preoccupations and the *business of life*, we can experience "a perpetual turning and returning inward, to figure out what our next move is."[15] Mindfulness in times of grief can lift this veil of preoccupations and show us that there is, in fact, more to life and more connections than we could previously see.

PHOTOGRAPHIC EQUIVALENT

While symbols in the grief journey often represent messages and relationships, photographic Equivalents reflect one's own inner emotional processes. Associations triggered by your environment are formally referred to as "Equivalents," a photographic phenomenon first described by American photographer Alfred Stieglitz in the context of his photographs of clouds. Stieglitz observed that objects in our visual field have the propensity to evoke feelings. He described his own experience of photographing clouds and experiencing the same sensations, or feelings, that he felt when he listened to classical music. His approach focused on that which moved him as an internal emotional experience, as he said, "It is only after I have put down an equivalent of what has moved me that I can even begin to think about its meaning."[16] In this way, he created parables through speech and visual image—Equivalents—of his own deeply felt experiences of life.

In 1955, after Stieglitz's death, Dorothy Norman, a close friend, wrote an article for *Aperture Magazine* where she shared a collection of his quotes and letters and her personal anecdotes that she had collected over the years. She wrote, "It was as though whenever Stieglitz would witness a moment of light, it would awaken within him a kind of miracle of response—a responsive soaring of his own sense of wonder beyond darkness—an act of faith." Norman further described the way in which Stieglitz's inner emotional experience informed his approach to photography.

> He would, in a sense, photograph those moments that would enlighten him about the cause—the nature—of his own heartache before he had entirely understood it himself, either in personal or universal terms. His photographs may be said to be what he himself felt all works of art must be: an act of paying homage to that moment of illumination, that moment in whose presence one knows most deeply that there is a center beyond centers that cannot be known, that cannot be touched, that cannot be defiled, yet that alone seems to make life meaningful.

Minor White, a fine arts photographer, expanded on Stieglitz's notion of the photographic Equivalent and suggested that the way in which things are seen can reflect a person's being and consciousness.[17] His experience surfaced through visual metaphors and described different levels of equivalence. First, he refers to Equivalence as a visual experience, not an object or state:

> If the individual viewer realizes that for him what he sees in a picture corresponds to something within himself—that is, the photograph mirrors something in himself—then his experience is some degree of Equivalence.[18]

White's second level of Equivalence refers to looking at the image and his "correspondence to something that he knows about himself."[19] The third level of Equivalence is when the viewer doesn't see the photograph anymore but remembers the photograph. Because we tend to remember things that we want to remember, the focus is on the inner sense of emotion and experience through recollection. At a basic level, photographic Equivalence is like a mirror that reflects something back to you. A photographic Equivalent made while grieving not only renders a deeper understanding but can also be self-validating and have a grounding effect. This is because photographs offer something tangible that is seen, held, and can be returned to.

In chapter 4, Avery reflected on their image of the knotted-up sticks that washed up on shore. They connected it with their internal experience of feeling emotional knots and continued by observing shapes in the image that matched the qualities of their lived experience. They also described a visual metaphor between their inner experience of wanting to accept and not resist their feelings as they come up with that of the "waves lapping up on the shore."

> That tangle really spoke to the knots that I felt like I've had to untangle emotionally. There are pointy, sharp bits and then there's smoother, happier memories that feel better underfoot, so to speak. The rocky angles to trip on that can be stumbling blocks along the path. And then there's a way to pick away through it.
>
> But there's no getting rid of any part of it. It's all part of the process. Just trying to take thoughts and feelings as they come, kind of like waves lapping up on a shore against the riverbank and just whatever comes up, it is valid. And keeping that in mind and trying not to fight against it. (Photo 4.1, page 41)

White understood the photographic process to be composed of three phases: creativity, growth, and vision.[20] This process reflects White's belief that seeing is both internal and external. White expressed his understanding of photography as a path toward spiritual awareness and often described a spiritual aspect to the process as he said, "With the theory of Equivalence, photographers everywhere are given a way of learning to use the camera in relation to the mind, heart, viscera and spirit of human beings." When a photograph functions for a given person as an equivalent, at that moment and for that person the photograph acts as a symbol or metaphor for something that is beyond what was photographed.

When the photograph is a mirror
of the man
and the man is a mirror of the world
then spirit might take over.[21]

As you become visually attuned to your environment and photos are made with full awareness, there follows a space for deep reflection and the meaning-making process to unfold. You might notice that as you reflect on your photographs, qualities in the image represent internal experiences and aspects of yourself and your grief journey. This is the experience of participants, many of whom described how the practice helped them explore and understand their emotions.

Gracie James reflected on the image they made of the rusty metal gate, a remnant of the high school that was once there where their father worked. They noted that the gate represented something that was blocking them and considered their emotional experience that day as they made their way beyond that gate and continued to walk. They were moved internally to get beyond the "stuckness" of anxiety to the deeper, more vulnerable feelings underneath. They further reflected on the beaten trails in the image as a means of walking out the difficult feelings while they still could.

> The loneliness surfaced as I was moving. It's interesting to look back now at that gate and think that there's something blocking me. When I first started the walk, there was a lot of anxiety. I think in moving and in choosing images and in relating to the space got me out of that stuckness of anxiety. And then, what was that covering up? Just a deep, deep, deep, deep longing, and that kind of loneliness of "this is mine."
>
> I'm not a religious person, and I'm not particularly spiritual either. And I don't think that I've made things up; I mean, I know people say that they get tired of one-way conversations with the dead and really want to hear something. I do hear him, and I don't think it's my fantasy world. I think that I'm hearing an energy thread that has a depth, that has a distance to it, and there's points along the line where we can meet. Maybe that's why there's all these trails, literally walking to walk it out, to walk out the frustration, the anger, the sorrow. But also because I don't know how long this line is. I don't know; I like to think it's long. (Photo 4.12, page 58)

The images created while practicing the Within and Without Method create a map through grief because they help you understand where you are in the emotional landscape, and they help provide a path forward. Identifying photographic Equivalents in Steps 3 and 4 can help you understand how you feel. Seeing your emotional process reflected back to you through something you created is validating and can provide inner strength and movement forward in your grief journey. An important aspect of making images that might render an Equivalent is mindfulness. Mindfulness can help you let go of expectations and open you up to the present moment, which, in turn, can inspire attunement and yield a deeper understanding and connection with your images.

NOTES

1. Field and Filanosky, 2009.
2. Davis et al., 2007, p. 695.
3. Hibberd, 2013.
4. Neimeyer, 2016, p. 66.
5. Arnold, 2018.
6. e.g., Cooper et al., 2007; Lowey, 2008; Salmon et al., 2005; Shirai et al., 2009.
7. Cacciatore and Flint, 2012; Currier et al., 2006; Rushton et al., 2009.
8. Freeman, 2014, p. 57.
9. Colman, 2010.
10. Segal, 1952, pp. 201–202.
11. Jakoby, 2012.
12. Trungpa, 2008, p. 68.
13. Chen, 1997.
14. Jung, 1971.
15. Freeman, 2014.
16. Norman, 1955.
17. White, 1963.
18. Ibid., p. 17.
19. Ibid.
20. White et al, 1989.
21. Ibid., p. 58.

CHAPTER 6

Transformative Growth

One does not become enlightened by imagining figures of light, but by making the darkness conscious.

—CARL JUNG

WHILE PROCESSING THE DEATH OF A LOVED ONE WE OFTEN FACE PROfound spiritual dimensions that can inspire meaningful reflection and transformation. A belief that growth through difficult life experiences is possible and devotion toward that growth can, and often does, inspire a transformative journey. The practice outlined in this book is an invitation to face grief and death with a sense of openness and curiosity and knowledge that growth and transformation are likely outcomes. The Within and Without Method presents a creative method for befriending grief, connecting with individual spiritual practice, forming new meaning and insights, and gaining a renewed sense of self and others. Having undergone a transformative process, you can develop a new relationship with death and grief. You begin to understand that grief is not something you recover from or return from, but rather it is something that you are changed from. Your outlook and perceptions of life change as you allow a transformation to occur. The broken pieces that you once saw as grief can be transformed into a stunning mosaic.

BEFRIENDING GRIEF

Anxiety can surface when death is present, and the subsequent reaction can be a desire to structure things to reduce the anxiety and fear of the unknown.[1] The desire to control and keep busy becomes a way to avoid feeling the pain and fear of grief and loss. However, by avoiding the loss, you also avoid who you are and what is true for yourself on a deep, existential, and humanistic level. When you let go of fear and anxiety, you stop clinging and trying to control things. You loosen your grip (which decreases much of your suffering) and gain the ability to hold your grief differently. You can move away from rigidity and angst and be open to experiencing other aspects of your lived experience. Instead of focusing on the loss and subsequent grief as something that was *done* to you, you can refocus and shift to how you want to proceed in the wake of it. The shift in how one holds their grief can produce momentum toward transformation and experiencing more love, compassion, and gratitude.

You can mediate anxiety by gaining the ability to slow down, reassure yourself, and accept things as they are. In my research study, Judy described how mindful photography helped her to contemplate her current experience and choose how she wanted to proceed.

> Every time I took one of these pictures, I was motivated to take it because I was thinking this is a temporary situation I'm in. I'm not going to be here. I don't know when my friend's going to die. It looks like he's going faster than we ever thought. I can get myself anxious about that, or I can slow down. Mindful photography helped me to slow down.

When you slow down, you can grow increasingly aware of who you are and how you feel, which, in turn, can nurture the inner strength that is needed to confront your experience and choose how you want to perceive it. Janet emphasized this aspect of the phenomenon as she realized that she could choose hope rather than fear.

> What I want to do is live it all, every bit of it, all the inconsistencies. I want to enter in, not concerned about being consistent at all. Nothing about the situation in which we find ourselves right now is all bad.

Neither is it all good (with ALS, not by a long shot). But we can choose to see light, even if it's only a glimmer.

As you open to your aesthetic experience, cultivating what Dufrenne referred to as *sympathetic reflection* and Geiger described as *aesthetic attitude*, you learn to slow down and perceive your experience through feeling, perception, and reflection.[2] You can cultivate an aesthetic attitude in connection with your mindful photography practice, which, in turn, expands awareness and shines a light on other parts of your experience beyond fear and angst. Cultivating aesthetic perception through mindful photography while in grief can give rise to existential awareness, and that awareness, in turn, can give rise to a sense of gratitude. In other words, it is through the culmination of aesthetic perception and existential awareness that you can experience gratitude and a greater desire to be mindfully present.

The camera is a tool that can guide you into present-moment awareness; however, the images you create are what become the objects of reflection. While the pervasive knowledge of death and loss is present, as you slow down and reflect, the fear associated with the loss can shift toward a sense of gratitude. Janet continued her reflection, and poignantly described this aspect as she reflected on the image she had made of her dying husband's hand. In her recollection of making that image, she anticipated missing him; however, that grief quickly shifted to gratitude and a desire to stay mindfully present with him in that moment.

> Tal's hand, once so strong, resting, relaxed on the arm of the rocking chair. Now, that sight overwhelmed me. I shall miss him so much. BUT I don't want to borrow all that now; I want to enjoy right now, this moment. I don't want to miss this, what we have right here, right now. (Photo 6.1, page 82)

Grief is a natural part of life and being human. Choosing to embrace that journey can lead us toward what Rummet described as "Sophia wisdom": consciously befriending our feelings and issues around death so that we can live comfortably with our mortality with neither avoidance

Photo 6.1. Janet, hand. Photo courtesy of author.

nor preoccupation, seeing life and death as integral parts of an infinite, unending flow.[3] Learning to hold grief with a sense of gratitude and love can help you befriend your feelings around death and loss. This new relationship with death and loss offers inner peace, but it can also be a source of inspiration. There are many people, including myself, that are inspired by their grief journey, many of whom feel called to help others. If you can manage to get beyond the suffering of loss, life seems to open. Offering to others opens your heart, and openheartedness often leads to a sense of well-being that fends off states of depression and anxiety.[4]

Making photographic images becomes a process of discovery toward new insights, beyond the suffering of grief. In their explorative capacity, images prove to be objects of potential transformation. For instance, when I reflect on the image I had made of my grandmother's and my baby nephew's hands, I realize the impermanent, ever-changing, and inexhaustible quality of such images. Although the image did not change in its physical form, my relationship with it grew. Now when I look at the image, I connect it with an expanded life narrative that is not only mine but is a part of a collective journey. My perceptions of death, grief, and loss and my emotions toward them became less personal and more transpersonal. It is through such an expansion that the space for peace and freedom emerge. Symbolically, the image portrays the strength of my own faith as I become infused with the belief and felt sense that life is precious. I see that life is not meant to be grasped with a clenched fist so much as held with an open hand.

Continuing Bonds

We are intrinsically relational beings, learning and growing in relation to others. Grief can be a relational experience, and in many parts of the world, death and grief are embedded in a sense of relationality that is framed as a collective experience.[5] The notion of continuing bonds validates the relational perspective of death and grief by suggesting that maintaining a sense of connection and bond with your deceased loved one might support a healthy adjustment process.[6] Continuing a bond with your deceased loved one might be through visiting their grave, getting a memorial tattoo, continuing to celebrate their birthday, or it may involve religious and cultural rituals. It might mean connecting with objects that were once owned by or held some special meaning to your loved one. For instance, in chapter 4, Gracie James shared images of their father's prayer card, which they have kept in their wallet for years. While these are outward, physical forms of continuing a bond, you might also demonstrate an ongoing bond in a more inward-focused way. Internalized continuing bonds refer to experiences that primarily involve contemplation, reflection, and reminiscence.[7] In this way, the deceased is used as an internal secure base that can offer a sense of comfort and strength.

The Within and Without Method can be a practice or ritual that helps you maintain a connection with a loved one as they are dying or it can help you explore a continued bond after a loss. This aspect occurred in my research study as participants were moved to share their images with their dying loved one as a way to connect and maintain a bond. And in chapter 4, continuing bonds surfaced in the moments when participants created mindful photographs and, later, when they reflected on their images as symbolic portrayals of the relationship. Creating a symbolic connection with their loved one was a way in which they connected with their presence. Segal's view of symbol formation as a creative act honors the interdependent nature of life, relationships, and healing, and it highlights meaning as something that we can create versus something that is hidden—that which we must search for and hope we find.[8]

> Because symbols are embedded in a context of communication and can only develop in the context of a relationship, representing both relationships and objects, they are emergent in the sense that they exist within a complex web of interactions and multiple meanings, thus cannot be reduced back to any one object that they represent.[9]

Symbols are rich with meaning in part because they are undetermined. Much like a photograph, they are a living and growing thing in which new meanings accrue, never fully exhausting their symbolic potential. For example, the image I made of my grandmother's and nephew's hands is everchanging, and its connection and meaning will continue to evolve, just as I continue to evolve and grow. Symbolic images can serve as transitional objects of grief and offer you a sense of security and symbolic connection to your loved one that died. Your mindful photographs might reflect moments of connection with your deceased loved one and, later, upon reflection, gain even deeper significance.

Continuing a Bond with a Deceased Loved One

In chapter 4, Josh explored his grief associated with the recent death of his grandmother. He reflected on the image he made of the house at the end of the block with Christmas lights. The fog in the photograph symbolized for him all the unknowns that surround death while the Christmas lights that lit up that dark and foggy night symbolized the special relationship he shared with his grandmother.

> I saw the house at the end of the road more visible due to the Christmas lights still fitted around the home. It made me feel connected to

my grandmother. As a child, she was always a light in the darkness that was my childhood. Regardless of the dark trauma and pain I was experiencing she was always there to comfort me, tend my wounds, and remind me that love still existed in the world. I knew that no matter how much darkness I had to run through, she'd be there at the end of it. (Photo 4.6, page 48)

In the interview for Step 4, Josh further reflected on the image he made and its connection to him, his relationships, and his grief journey. Not only did the image represent the caring relationship with his grandmother, but it also told him something. The symbolic nature of the image relayed a message of connection and love and reflected the continued bond he has with his grandmother.

The answer that I felt like I was getting was maybe to a question that I didn't even know I had, and that was where do I connect myself to love? And that night it was like, "Well, Grandma." I always felt safe with her.

I think that the photo specifically was telling me that even with the unknowns of death, even with the disconnect that we often feel when someone dies, that there is still that thread that keeps us connected and together, that through the veil of unknowns, I still have a connection to her, and that connection was the love that she provided me, the love that I still feel.

Also in chapter 4, Ruth reflected on the image she made of the late-blooming roses that caught her eye. She talked about the significance that roses have in her life, including a connection to her mother. She also mentioned that the image was relaying a message of feeling cared for.

Roses hit me in a lot of different ways because my mother loved roses, and sometimes, that was a nickname for me: Rosa. I even have a little ceramic rose that belonged to her. So, I had a lot of messages come into my brain when I saw them. Messages of connection.

I think it's telling me that I'm not totally uncared for or unloved, because sometimes, that's what it feels like when I'm working so hard and taking care of everything. I'm associating feeling cared for because it's pleasant and it's not hurting me. I feel cared for instead of feeling hurt. It's pleasant, not unpleasant. (Photo 4.11, page 56)

Continuing a Bond with a Dying Loved One

Family members who are anticipating a death often begin to distance themselves from one another, including the dying person, in an attempt to cope.[10] The process of sharing your mindful photographs with a dying loved one might be a way for you to stay connected and continue a bond, even as their health declines. Janet noted the sharing process that unfolded with her dying husband and the photographs that she shared with him. She talked about how they had always been active together but have had to find new ways to connect since the illness. Janet's sharing of her photographs with her dying husband became a way to connect and bond throughout the experience.

> We've been having to find ways to do things together because physically we used to be very active. We hiked and canoed and fished and traveled. Physically, he can't do that. He loved this project because he's wanted to see the pictures, and he's wanted to see what I had to draw from. I haven't shared the journal entries, but I have shared the photographs.

Although my research study did not exclusively focus on the sharing of photographs, it did question whether a sharing process might create better bonds between family, friends, and community who are anticipating a death.[11] Participants in the study who chose to share their images either with their dying loved one or with a friend or family member did so as a way to connect. During the interview, Judy reflected on her desire to share the mindful photographs she made with her friend who was dying as a way to connect and continue their bond.

> Taking these pictures and wanting to share them with him was a way of saying, "You have your experience, and I have mine, and we actually can join in our being vulnerable and our not having control over what's going on. We only have control of our being here with each other."

Sharon Salzberg, a Buddhist and meditation teacher, said that, "vulnerability in the face of change is what we share, whatever our present condition."[12] This is especially true when we are faced with grief and death. Shared vulnerability can be a point of connection if we can lean into our experience with a sense of openness. When you make photographs from a place of attunement and connection, they reflect aspects of you. Sharing images with your dying loved one with the intention to connect becomes an intimate gesture that can help maintain a bond and possibly open up more discussions around the impending loss. In this way, sharing images might also be a way to co-construct meaning of the loss before your loved one dies. Mindful photographs created in bereavement can serve as symbolic representations and a point of connection with your deceased loved one. Reflecting on your images and their significance can help you understand how the relationship with your loved one is still meaningful and can evolve as a continued bond.

> *Death has nothing to do with going away.*
> *The sun sets. The moon sets.*
> *But they are not gone.*

> —RUMI[13]

SACRED OUTLOOK

The experience of loss or an impending loss can evoke a cultivation of one's spirituality in the meaning-making process. It is through the human struggle that we learn to let go of attachments and experience the true nature of life: impermanence. Death and grief can inspire one to transcend the impervious structure of existence and embrace a shift toward transpersonal values and identity, beyond the ego-self. Transpersonal psychologist Dr. Frances Vaughan said that the basic characteristics of the transpersonal Self are wisdom and compassion and that we know we are "awake to the transpersonal Self when we feel peace."[14] Other characteristics of the transpersonal Self that are relevant to the Within and Without Method are intuition, creativity, receptiveness, openness, connection, love, and inspiration.

Valle and Mohs also outline characteristics that "point the way or serve as windows to the spiritual realm," one of which is confidence. They described confidence as "feeling an inner strength" and "strong, not because we regard someone else as weak, but rather, because we trust our experience."[15] You can develop inner strength, as well as other transpersonal qualities, by confronting and exploring your grief experience for yourself. Inner strength gives rise to authentic insight as you trust your own perceptions and gain a greater sense of awareness. Chögyam Trungpa described this way of knowing in relation to a camera's aperture as thus:

> You let yourself go a little further; you open yourself. It is like a camera aperture: your lens is open at that point. Then you can see things, and they reflect into your state of mind.[16]

Through a reflective process, inner strength grows as you gain a sense of confidence and accomplishment regarding your mindful photography practice and efforts in exploring your own grief experience. You gain the ability to validate and reassure yourself through the process of gleaning meaning from your photographs, and a sense of empowerment and inner strength are nurtured as you perceive and express your own experience. In my research study, Janet expressed inner strength as she reflected on her photographs, describing herself as being "embraced and strengthened."[17] Furthermore, the practice acted as a framework that enhanced her own ability to function and thrive through her grief journey.

> It doesn't have to be the framework of the dogma or the orthodoxy of a faith, but the framework of thinking that there is creation, and there is brokenness, and there is hope, and there is redemption and all of that. I can think through that process, that creation-to-redemption process. That's a wonderful framework to use. That's what I see now. I am reminded of one of the photographs I submitted last week, the one of the moonflower beginning its twining up the trellis. When I made it, I was thinking of my own sort of desperate clinging, saying I was tethered, connected. As I have continued to muse on that image, however, I realize now that I am not simply tethered but that I have a framework

Photo 6.2. Janet, trellis. Photo courtesy of author.

on which, within which, to function, to live, to thrive. That to me is a somehow hardier, a more substantial outlook or attitude. I was clinging when I made that image; I am embraced and strengthened now. (Photo 6.2, page 89)

Pain is a natural part of life. You cannot simply jump over your grief. You must be willing to open to your pain and grapple with the experience to move toward acceptance, gratitude, and peace. As described by one participant, "I can let the camera help me grapple with how I feel." By opening up, you can stop clinging to the pain of loss and gain access to inner strength—a confidence that grows from your ability to explore your grief. Authentic insight and wisdom can arise as you create meaning based on direct experience and trust yourself through the process. While reflecting on the image Janet made of her feet in the grass, she described the image in contrast to the one she made at the beginning of that photo walk, an image of stacked stone. She said that the stacked stone symbolized her feelings of angst and feeling *stacked up and heavy*. However, by the end of that photo walk, she described a shift toward peace and comfort, as symbolized by her feet in the grass. The insights gained through her direct experience and the reflective process helped her realize that movement and growth were possible.

> You've got to look at it [the emotional experience] and work with it to get it to move. And the same thing with the photography and with the moments of my days now. I have to be present for them, and I have to participate in them, or I'm not going to get to that point of feeling my feet in the grass and comforted. I can't get from angst to comforted unless I'm willing to participate and look at it. I just took off my shoes and stood in this tall, cool, soft grass; there was comfort there. (Photo 6.3)

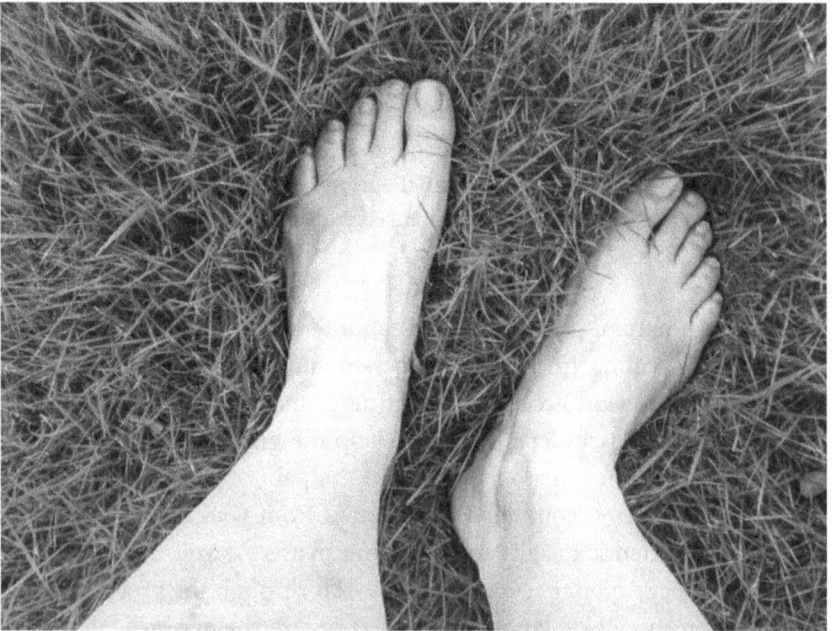

Photo 6.3. Janet, feet. Photo courtesy of author.

When you realize that growth is possible, you might feel "inspiration and enthusiasm come together, a true passion for life, an unfolding authenticity and a passionate search for truth that uses the events of life to more deeply investigate the nature of your inner essence or soul."[18] A desire for depth and meaning move us beyond ourselves and our own suffering. Once you get beyond yourself and open to something larger, you are introduced to a world beyond attachment, wherein lies a potential shift from desire toward devotion. Tending to your grief can become a devotional experience.

As transpersonal aspects of truth-seeking and meaning-making transpire, a more expansive view and life narrative emerge. Beyond understanding your grief as "your own," you begin to understand it as a collective journey, where you are neither alone nor separate. In chapter 4, Josh was moved to reflect on the journey of life and death as something we all make and the feeling of interconnectedness that is experienced through making such an awareness. Furthermore, he described how existential confusion can be a prerequisite for having greater connection in our lives.

> I remember being grateful and feeling like this whole cycle that we go through, with life and death, birth and growing up . . . it was a rainy day, it was this rejuvenation . . . and, these things have to happen. We have to have rain to have new growth, and we have to rely on the earth for sustenance and, to a certain degree, shelter. I mean, that's how we get bricks and wood for building houses. So, there was this sense of interconnectedness with the world around me.
>
> What it reaffirmed for me was life. Grief, it turns everything upside down; my own experience is that it can make things not make sense. This existential confusion we have about why this is happening, and as we process through that, inadvertently, sometimes we get reconnected with the life that we have.

Devotion as "sacred outlook" in context to grief is profound acceptance.[19] If you can learn to shift your outlook and perception of grief in the moment and suffer less and less, *sacred outlook* becomes the foundation for transforming grief. Buddhist scholar Gaylon Ferguson discussed sacred outlook in relation to the Buddhist tantric view and practice.[20] He said that sacred outlook, also referred to as pure perception, sees a sacred world, and that it is the fresh and direct experience of ourselves and others, all beings, animate and inanimate. Freeman described a similar process in relation to the way one's attention and responsibility are called forth by the Other.

> Insofar as the Other is that which draws us out of ourselves, takes us somewhere beyond our customary preoccupations and concerns, *moves us*, it may be human or non-human, animate or inanimate. Along the lines being drawn here, it is not so much the *object* that defines what is Other as the *process*.[21]

The degree to which we can be *drawn out of ourselves* is a combination of openness and attention toward *Other*. Because grief can break us open, it can position us toward experiencing transformation. The process that unfolds might be experienced as transcendent in the way that Freeman described it as a function of release, our defenses being broken down, "revealing the 'real self' in its primal givenness; it is the 'sense' one may get on realizing the full depth and measure of one's inner life."[22] Viktor Frankl, a well-known Austrian psychiatrist and Holocaust survivor, contemplated the "intensification of inner life" that helped prisoners stay alive. In his book *Man's Search for Meaning*, he talks about a moment in the camps that he was moved to converse silently with his wife—who was physically not present. He considered the transcendental power of love and how relationships can still serve as a source of strength beyond space and time.

> Love goes very far beyond the physical person of the beloved. It finds its deepest meaning in his spiritual being, his inner self. Whether or not he is actually present, whether or not he is still alive at all, ceases somehow to be of importance.[23]

As you journey through the internal landscape of grief, feelings can shift, making space for new connections. Gracie James reflected on the image they made of a beaten trail in the open field where some of their father's ashes were spread. They were moved to imagine the present relationship and bond with their father, as symbolized in that field. In their journal, they wrote, "We are a part of something larger. You and I are light and dirt." As Gracie James continued to reflect on that image, they felt a shift. Insight emerged as they recognized an embodied presence alongside a new way of seeing and being.

> My feelings shift. The loss is something that is known in the cells, its feeling ever-changing, now known as a wave to ride. When you stare into the ocean, you learn to distinguish all layers of color and light as you give in to seeing in a new way of shape and movement.

When they reflected on their image and journal entry in the interview, they recognized the many layers still present and said, "I'm not just sad and mad. There's a lot more going on." They reflected deeper on the comment in their journal entry "loss is known in the cells" and shared a story about their grandmother (their father's mother), who recently visited them in a dream. It was through that sharing and reflection that the comment gained an expansive meaning and understanding. Similar to what Frankl described, it is not just grief that is embodied and held in the cells, but it is also the strength and care from those relationships.

> My dad's mother visited me last week in a dream. I woke up thinking about her and this thing about cellular memory and how she held it together, held the family in a true matriarch style. And I thought, "Oh, I can do this. My grandma was tough. I don't have to fix anything. I have to take care. I have to take care. There's ways I want things to go, but I don't know if that's how they'll go, but I need to take care along the way, moment by moment by moment." And I think that that's something that I didn't come up with, I think that's in my cells, and is good to acknowledge.

The Within and Without Method offers a framework to help ground you through a journey that can often feel groundless and unsteady. It can gently guide you through exploring difficult emotions that come with grief, and it might also inspire you to consider the ever-evolving relationship with your deceased loved one. The creative process inspires a sense of curiosity and wonder that can give rise to deeper reflections, rendering transpersonal awareness and perhaps transcendent experience.

NOTES

1. Valle and Mohs, 2006.
2. Dufrenne,1973; Geiger, 1986.
3. Rummet, 2006, p. 111.
4. Kabat-Zinn, 1990, 2004.
5. McCarthy et al., 2023.
6. Klass et al., 1996.
7. Field and Filanosky, 2009.
8. Segal, 1952.
9. Ibid.
10. Rolland, 2004.
11. Thomas, 2016.
12. Salzberg, 1999.
13. Rumi and Nicholson, 2004.
14. Walsh and Vaughan, 1993, p. 43.
15. Valle and Mohs, 2006, p. 81.
16. Trungpa, 2008, p. 158.
17. Thomas, 2016.
18. Valle & Mohs, 2006, p. 86.
19. Marshall, 1999.
20. Ferguson, 2023.
21. Freeman, 2014, p. 113.
22. Ibid., p. 164.
23. Frankl, 1985.

CHAPTER 7

Therapeutic Photography

The question is not what you look at—but how you look and whether you see.

—Henry David Thoreau

Mindful photography brings the opportunity to become present in times of change, to witness the passing of another and be open to transformation. Self-guided use of Steps 1 through 3 of the Within and Without Mindful Photography Method can help you access this ritual and presence for yourself, allowing space for peace and healing. However, the full cathartic process is accessed when joining a group of other grievers to complete Step 4 together and with a therapist.

The ability to explore and express your grief in communion with others can be a healing ingredient. However, because Western society has evolved to be largely death denying, the communal aspect of healing is often missed. Only a few generations ago, death was very much a part of life as families, friends, and communities cared for their dying loved ones at home and took care of their loved ones' bodies in the hours and days after death. Now, in the United States, we see death as an emergency and call the professionals—doctors, nurses, police, emergency workers, and funeral staff.[1] They hurry our loved ones' bodies from homes or hospital rooms into designated, chilled death spaces. They dig and fill the graves for us and drive our loved ones, alone, to the crematories. By removing ourselves from those processes, we lose out on the communal aspects that come with them.

Creating more opportunities for grievers and those anticipating a loss to communally explore, share, and support one another's journey can have a transformative impact on individuals and communities. In this larger social context, these opportunities can humanize and destigmatize talking about death and grief and inspire a shift in attitudes. Rather than seeing death as a failure of some sort, we can understand death as an integral part of being human. Thus, grief can be understood as a symptom of being human and evidence of love, not a sign of weakness.

When facilitated in groups, within a safe and therapeutic environment, the Within and Without Mindful Photography Method can evoke a sense of shared vulnerability and compassion among group members. The combination of sharing on this deeper level and feeling seen by others who personally understand grief creates fertile ground for transformation and healing to occur both individually and systemically.

HEALING RITUAL

Photography has been used as a therapeutic tool for some time now; however, it has grown significantly in recent years with the advent of the phone camera. It is described both informally as a self-guided therapeutic practice and formally as a therapeutic technique involving a therapist.

Therapeutic photography is any self-initiated activity that is self-conducted and centered on photography but includes no formal therapist.[2] Steps 1 through 3 outlined in chapter 3 offer an overview of mindful photography as a self-initiated practice to help ground you and begin the initial stages of reflection and processing your grief.

Making space in your life to practice therapeutic photography can be a grief ritual where you honor the presence of grief and open up to your unique journey. Making space for ritual refers to both outer space and inner space because you not only make time in your day to practice but you also intentionally make the inner space to reflect. Healing rituals bring together the inner world and the outer world to create a sense of restoration, meaning, and wholeness. Grief rituals are powerful because they support healthier feelings, attitudes, and behaviors for accepting the reality of a loss.[3] Ji Hyang Padma, a Buddhist scholar-practitioner, has written extensively about the power of ritual and consciousness.

> Rituals are embodied narratives. We need these embodied narratives, because as humans we need story. We are designed and driven to make meaning of our lives through the symbols of narrative. They affect the flow of energy and information within the encounter, to bring about a change of consciousness and deep mind/body healing.[4]

Separate from the self-initiated practice of therapeutic photography is "Photo Therapy," a term coined by Judy Weiser, which refers to a formal therapeutic modality that utilizes a myriad of specific techniques guided by a therapist.[5] In general, the use of photography in therapeutic sessions aims to facilitate the individual's ability to recognize and express emotions and promote deeper understanding.[6] And, because the parts of the brain that process visual information are evolutionarily older than the parts that process verbal information, images evoke deeper elements of human consciousness than words alone.[7] Thus, integrating visual elements, such as photographs, into therapy can be extremely beneficial.

Photographs, when integrated into psychotherapy, bring to the interactive therapy sessions a concrete object, a symbol—a photograph that can be perceived and worked with together.[8] Because photographs reflect your reality and also leave room for interpretation and meaning, photo reflection can be an approachable way to process your thoughts and feelings in therapy. Furthermore, photographs can inspire meaning-making by providing contextual richness in triggering individuals' unique memories and working through them by visual storytelling.[9] In chapter 4, you may have noticed elements of this that surfaced for participants who, in the interview, recalled memories from the past and were moved to integrate the past into their present reality and meaning-making process. In particular, this tends to take place in bereavement when the griever is drawn toward remembrance and a desire for a continued bond.

The Within and Without Method is flexible as it integrates a self-guided mindful photography practice and a facilitated therapeutic technique. Step 4, "Authentic Insight," can be facilitated in therapy and in therapeutic environments such as support groups. Although this is not a training manual for Step 4, this chapter offers you an understanding on how the method can be transformative in therapeutic environments. Subsequent training on the method are offered for those interested in facilitating support groups and integrating it into therapy. Overall, this approach embraces grievers with agency as they explore and share what is meaningful for them. In group settings, a sense of connection, validation, and empowerment support the healing journey as group members open up to both share and bear witness.

REFLECTION GROUPS

Within and Without Mindful Photography reflection group sessions focus on supporting those who are experiencing grief and loss related to bereavement, caregiving, terminal illness, and other major life transitions. The reflection groups are organized by type of loss or life transition and provide an opportunity for group members to share and reflect on their mindful photographs and explore their grief narratives with others who are traversing a similar type of loss. Each group session builds on the previous and focuses on learning the practice steps as they have been meaningfully adjusted for a supportive group environment.

More specifically, groups typically meet once a week for four to six sessions and can also be integrated in a retreat or workshop setting. The first group session is based on Step 1, "Opening Up." It is an introduction to the practice of mindfulness and participants are encouraged to practice mindfulness walks without their camera. Because the practice is being applied in a group, Opening Up is not just a matter of opening to the practice; it is also opening up to the group process. Because people can feel self-conscious and reluctant to share in groups, it's imperative that a safe and nonjudgmental environment be created that is encouraging and supportive of each unique journey. A benefit of integrating mindfulness into healing groups is it brings members into the present moment and helps soften anxiety and fear. This sets the stage for a therapeutic environment where a sense of compassion and connection is cultivated.

As I mentioned, this method is facilitated not only for bereavement but also for other kinds of losses and life transitions. Most recently, I trained a volunteer at Alzheimer's San Diego, a nonprofit with a mission to enhance the quality of life of those affected by all dementias. The wide range of programs that they offer include support for those caring for a loved one with dementia and Alzheimer's. Over the course of several months, I trained Robin, a seasoned volunteer, to facilitate a Within and Without Mindful Photography reflection group. Robin had a personal relationship with Alzheimer's as she witnessed her father's decline some years ago. She is both exceptionally compassionate for those traversing such a loss and knowledgeable about the disease and its unique implications on caregivers. She is also a professional photographer, which presented some unique training aspects since mindful photography is quite different in terms of the overall process and intention. She became an excellent facilitator, joining with the group and creating a safe and non-judgmental environment that fostered curiosity, openness, restoration, and meaningful insights.

Feedback through recorded quotes, interviews, and surveys reported that group sessions presented a unique and creative way for caregivers to gain a deeper understanding of themselves and their feelings while also feeling seen, validated, empowered, and restored. Sara Moller, the Alzheimer's San Diego Social Activities Coordinator, assisted Robin by observing the sessions and making field notes. At the end of the program, she remarked how transformational the group was for caregivers (care partners) and how it shifted their perceptions and increased a sense of gratitude and empowerment.

I had the honor of observing the facilitation of the Mindful Photography program offered for our care partners. The four-week program was powerful because not only did it offer support, but it also transformed each person's "lens" and way of seeing their role as a care partner and their relationship with their loved one.

The practice outlined by Dr. Jessica Thomas offered a gentle and creative path toward empowerment as care partners became aware of their ability to choose how they want to perceive their experiences, create meaning, and gain insights through the world of mindful photography. During the course of the four weeks, we saw significant shifts in perspective, as care partners transitioned from feeling frustrated in their current situations, to feeling gratitude for the present moment. One of our care partners emphasized, "This program has truly changed how I see life. I am a much happier person now" at the end of our four weeks. I could not recommend Dr. Thomas's Mindful Photography program more. We are so grateful to have had the opportunity to experience the wonderful program.

Group members were inspired to see things differently and consider new perspectives. A salient theme that surfaced and gained momentum for members was the idea of "changing your lens." One member remarked, "I gained a different perspective I've been struggling to grab onto for a long time—change the lens you're looking through to see something differently." Openness and curiosity grew for members as they became more acquainted with the practice and comfortable in the group setting. Here are a few exemplars, followed by additional insights gleaned from group sessions.

Photo 7.1. Shadow. Photo courtesy of author.

Photo 7.2. Pavement. Photo courtesy of author.

Step 3. Emotional Resonance. My shadow kept getting in the way as I moved this way and that until I thought to stop and let me be a part of what I was searching for. (Photo 7.1, page 100)

Step 4. Authentic Insight Group Reflection. It makes you think about your situation, and you see that there are good things. You see asphalt, and you think it's so ugly, but it's not. It's texture. Even when it's not attractive, there's something in there. (Photo 7.2)

Another theme that surfaced for members in their journal entries and in group reflections was a desire for control while also feeling the need to let go and accept the present moment. Related to this was the experience of fear of what's to come countered with the realization that fear was a barrier to enjoying the present. The following are some quotes noted from the group reflection that transpired while reflecting on their images.

With our partners, we've been given this journey, and we want to control it. As I'm taking a photo of the tree, I say there's no depth in here. As an artist, I'm always manipulating the image, but it's also that way in life. We want to be able to do things to control this.

I like everything to just be so. I want my life to just be "so," but it's not. I'm still trying to lean towards that acceptance, knowing that my life is going to have these crooked turns, but I don't know what's ahead.

I find myself fearing what hasn't happened yet, and I'm missing all of the good things going on right now.

I feel like I'm having to let go of my husband, sooner than I have to. I want to protect him from knowing too much and getting hurt from it.

Topics related to death, grief, and loss remain taboo topics and are largely avoided in Western society. People can often feel isolated in part because they do not feel they can talk about their experiences. A sense of safety inspired members to open up to their own feelings and to the group. The sharing process that unfolded in group sessions promoted curiosity. Self-consciousness and uncertainty melted away as members leaned into present-moment awareness. In their concluding survey, one member remarked, "What stood out most is the amount of anxiety people carry and how I saw it released throughout the group sessions." The climate of shared vulnerability awakened new ways of seeing themselves and their lived experiences as caregivers.

I am not a talker. I surprised myself by talking and sharing my feelings.

It motivated me to speak up and share my thoughts and view things differently.

This class has made me feel so safe. It has allowed me to look at things differently to have an opportunity to change.

We have so much in common and yet so many ways of dealing with a similar situation.

Seeing how we share this journey, but we all walk a different path. We selected different pictures but, through reflection and discussion, saw similar feelings and experiences.

A relational aspect of mindfulness in groups is moment-to-moment attention to the living reality of the other—their words, voice, feelings, expressions, body language, and so on.[10] Group members cultivate the awareness of movement, moments of turning toward and away, informed by the intention to return to connection. The object of investigation is each member's connection to whatever arises in the moment. Through this connection, members become aware of their own and the others' reality. The relational aspects of mindfulness that unfold make for a co-creative journey where the interdependent nature of existence can be intuitively and experientially realized.

The group facilitator, Robin Harris, attended to the flow of the relationships and the movement of consciousness as group members reflected on their images with the group. Members shifted in and out from their own inner experience to that of the group's. Her ability to stay meaningfully present and aware created a safe holding space for group members. They were able to freely explore their lived experience as caregivers, this season of life, and the full breadth of feelings and thoughts. Here was the summation from Robin:

Facilitating the Within and Without Mindful Photography reflection group for caregivers who are supporting their loved ones with Alzheimer's was a profoundly rewarding experience, marked by a poignant transformation in their mindset. Witnessing these caregivers shift from a place of frustration and sadness to appreciation and gratitude has been nothing short of inspiring. Guiding these resilient women through mindful photography and group reflection allowed them to find solace amidst the everyday challenges they face. Through the lens of mindful photography, they have discovered a renewed appreciation for the beauty and significance of the relationships they hold so dear.

It was a privilege to facilitate this transformative journey, providing a supportive outlet that empowered each group member to navigate their caregiver role with a newfound sense of mindfulness and gratitude.

The positive impact of the group was not just experienced by the group members; it was also experienced by the facilitator, Robin, and the group assistant, Sarah. As a clinician and group facilitator myself, I have found Within and Without groups to be transformative because they tend to be invigoratingly positive and meaningful. By the end of facilitating sessions, I feel awestruck. This aspect of the method is important because it creates a sustainable environment for facilitators. Rather than feeling emotionally and psychologically depleted, facilitators can also benefit by feeling inspired and connected.

HEALING IN COMMUNION

Because humans live and thrive in community and connection, healing and transformative growth are social phenomena where families, friends, colleagues, and others impact (and are impacted by) the individual and where healing can be socially redemptive.[11] The late scholar and author bell hooks said, "Rarely, if ever, are any of us healed in isolation. Healing is an act of communion." By exploring your grief journey in communion with others, you disrupt an expectation that grief should be masked and hidden. By engaging in a shared process and connecting with others, we can demystify the individualistic notion of death and grief and, instead, open up to connection, vulnerability, support, and transformation. The space and conversation can be transformed from "I am experiencing this" to "We are experiencing this," and in that process, a humanizing and collective healing experience is fostered.[12] In this way, grief does not have to be an isolated journey; rather, it can be imbued with social connection and meaning.

Meaning-making does not happen in isolation; we shape—and are shaped by—the environment and relationships around us. Group therapy with a focus on meaning-making can offer insight into the systemic nature of meaning-making processes. For example, one study that facilitated a meaning-based group for uncomplicated grief found that an important benefit for members was the feeling of being bonded by their shared feelings of loss.[13] However, simultaneously, group members also understood their grief as unique. The universality and differences of their grief were held together and what emerged was a norm of valuing the diversity of grief within the group. Furthermore, the group became a place for sharing aspects of grief that could not easily be shared with other social networks.

Grief support groups can create the space that is needed to imagine community as conditions for healing. Being able to commune with others who share a similar experience can provide support for people to communicate with openness and authenticity. Furthermore, exercising shared vulnerability creates an intimate space that can deepen a well of compassion for yourself and others. Support groups are also a place where healing rituals and reflective practices can be expanded, harnessing the healing intentions of its members and creating shared transformational experiences. Perhaps communal healing spaces, such as support groups, can act as a sacred threshold. Padma illustrates this thought in the text, *Field of Blessings*:

> Rituals provide a vivid embodied and relational liminal space, a threshold between the physical and archetypal worlds. Through this liminal space, the power of the present moment can be fully utilized for personal and shared transformation.[14]

Exploring and sharing your own grief narrative might invite others to talk about theirs and encourage a society where death, dying, and grief are more openly talked about. Therapeutic photography and group photo reflection can serve as a vehicle for grievers to explore, express, and heal in communion with others. It can help grievers talk about difficult emotions that are largely denied, avoided, and invalidated while supporting momentum toward healing and transformation.

Those traversing grief related to a stigmatized death are especially vulnerable to isolation because their grief is often compounded by negative social responses and judgments. Their grief becomes devalued, depriving them of the opportunity to share their experiences with others and garner social support.[15] For example, those that lose a loved one to suicide, substance overdose, gang violence, or so on are at risk of feeling a sense of shame, humiliation, and self-blame. Creating nonjudgmental spaces for these grievers to explore, express, and share their grief journeys in communion with others is especially needed. I envision that Within and Without Mindful Photography reflection groups might create such conditions where these grief journeys are humanized and meaningful.

Connecting with and witnessing the grief of others in a therapeutic environment can increase compassion for our shared humanity. Furthermore, opening up and sharing your grief journey, or public grieving, may be purposed as "grief activism" intended to raise awareness and overcome stigmas associated with death and grief. For instance, sharing my story in the introduction was in part to commune with readers and also to humanize and destigmatize conversations on death and grief. Sharing your journey can be an act of generosity and love that has a ripple effect across generations.

NOTES

1. Jones, 2019.
2. Natoli and Suler, 2011.
3. Sas and Coman, 2016.
4. Padma, 2021, p. 43.
5. Weiser, 2018.
6. Halkola, 2009.
7. Harper, 2002.
8. Loewenthal, 2013.
9. Kim, 2016.
10. Germer, Siegel, and Fulton, 2016.
11. Ginwright, 2015.
12. Castrellón et al., 2021.
13. MacKinnon et al., 2016.
14. Padma, 2021, p. 47.
15. Doka, 1999.

Conclusion

*Love empowers us to live fully and die well. Death becomes, then, not
an end to life but a part of living.*

—BELL HOOKS

THE DIGITAL AGE HAS BROUGHT ABOUT A WORLDWIDE EVOLUTION OF
the integration of photography into our daily lives. Digital cameras, such
as the phone camera, allow us to document and remember all sorts of
experiences. When used intentionally, as this book points out, photography can also be used as a therapeutic tool. The creative process of making
photographs and intentional reflection on those photographs before and
after a loss can help mitigate or alleviate negative aspects of grieving and
help you perceive your experiences in new ways.[1] Furthermore, sharing
those images can be a powerful way of communicating, expressing yourself, and connecting with friends, family, and community.

While my father's death will always be a traumatic event for me, it
is now paired with a deep well of compassion, gratitude, and wisdom. I
did not get the chance to tell him goodbye in a worldly sense, but I think
about him, talk to him, and notice him in meaningful and synchronis-
tic ways. I honor my grief experiences as wisdom gained when I host a
Within and Without Mindful Photography reflection group or train
a facilitator or teach courses on death and dying. Bit by bit, I contrib-
ute toward a systemic shift in our society where we can be more death
accepting rather than death denying and where there is more access to
social grief support rather than grief isolation. Ultimately, my hope is that
through this method, we can experience communal healing and share

it with others, creating ripples for a more conscious and compassionate society.

NOTE
1. Lister et al., 2008; Thomas, 2016.

Resources

For more information, please visit my website at Dr.JessicaThomas.com, which provides both death education and support. Beyond that, here is an outline of other organizations that are working to make death education and grief support more accessible.

Death Education Organizations
- NW Association of Death Education and Bereavement Support
- Portland Institute for Loss and Transition
- Association of Death Education and Counseling
- University of Bath Centre for Death and Society
- Death Salon
- Death Café
- Order of the Good Death
- Radical Death Studies

Grief Support Organizations
- Grief Share
- Dougy Center
- What's Your Grief?
- The Compassionate Friends

- SAVE: Suicide Awareness Voices of Education
- Zen Caregiving Project
- Coping With Loss

References

Arnold, C. (2018). *Using photo narrative to explore meaning reconstruction among bereaved university students* (Doctoral dissertation, Saybrook University).

Barthes, R. (1981). *Camera Lucida: Reflections on photography*. New York: Farrar, Straus, & Giroux.

Betensky, M. (1995). *What do you see?: Phenomenology of therapeutic art expression*. London: Jessica Kingsley.

Bijoux, D., and Myers, J. (2006). Interviews, solicited diaries and photography: "New" ways of accessing everyday experiences of place. *Graduate Journal of Asia-Pacific Studies, 4*(1), 44–64.

Bishop, S., Lau, M., Shapiro, S., Carlson, L., Anderson, N., Carmody, J., et al. (2004). Mindfulness: A proposed operational definition. *Clinical Psychology: Science and Practice, 11*(3), 230–41.

Bortorf, H. (1996). *The wholeness of nature: Goethe's way towards a science of conscious participation in nature*. Hudson, NY: Lindisfarne Press.

Boud, D. (2001). Using journal writing to enhance reflective practice. *New Directions for Adult and Continuing Education, 90*, 9–18.

Brown, K. W., Ryan, R. M., and Creswell, J. D. (2007). Mindfulness: Theoretical foundations and evidence for its salutary effects. *Psychological Inquiry, 18*(4), 211–37.

Brown, W. R., and Richard, M. (2004). Perils and promise in defining and measuring mindfulness: Observations from experience. *Clinical Psychology: Science and Practice, 11*(3), 242–48.

Cacciatore, J., and Flint, M. (2012). ATTEND: Toward a mindfulness-based bereavement care model. *Death Studies, 36*(1), 61–82.

Castrellón, L. E., Fernández, E., Rivarola, A. R. R., and López, G. R. (2021). Centering loss and grief: Positioning schools as sites of collective healing in the era of COVID-19. *Frontiers in Education, 6*, p. 636993.

Chang, F., Mullin, E., Trantham, S., Surrey, J., and Rappaport, L. (2013). *Mindfulness and the arts therapies: Theory and practice*. London: Jessica Kingsley.

Churchill, S, D., and Wertz, F., J. (2001). An introduction to phenomenological research in psychology: Historical, conceptual, and methodological foundations. In K. J. Schneider, J. F. T. Bugental, and J. F. Pierson (eds.), *The handbook of humanistic psychology: Leading edges in theory, research and practice* (pp. 247–62). Thousand Oaks, CA: Sage.

Colman, W. (2010). Mourning and the symbolic process. *Journal of Analytical Psychology*, *55*(2), 275–97.

Cooper, C., Balamurali, T. B., Selwood, A., and Livingston, G. (2007). A systematic review of intervention studies about anxiety in caregivers of people with dementia. *International Journal of Geriatric Psychiatry*, *22*(3), 181.

Creswell, J. (2012). *Qualitative inquiry and research design: Choosing among five approaches* (3rd ed.). Thousand Oaks, CA: Sage.

Currier, J. M., Holland, J. M., and Neimeyer, R. A. (2006). Sense-making, grief, and the experience of violent loss: Toward a meditational model. *Death Studies*, *30*(5), 40–3428.

Daaleman, T. P., Usher, B. M., Williams, S. W., Rawlings, J., and Hanson, L. C. (2008). An exploratory study of spiritual care at the end of life. *Annals of Family Medicine*, *6*(5), 406–11.

Davis, C. G., Wohl, M. J., and Verberg, N. (2007). Profiles of posttraumatic growth following an unjust loss. *Death Studies*, *31*(8), 693–712.

Doka, K. J. (1999). Disenfranchised grief. *Bereavement care*, *18*(3), 37–39.

Dufrenne, M. (1973). *The phenomenology of aesthetic experience*. Evanston, IL: Northwestern University Press.

Egan, R., MacLeod, R. J. C., McGee, R., Baxter, J., and Herbison, P. (2011). What is spirituality? Evidence from a New Zealand hospice study. *Mortality*, *16*(4), 307–24.

Ferguson, G. (2023). The power of Buddhist tantra. *The Lion's Roar*. Boulder, CO: Shambhala Publications.

Field, N. P., and Filanosky, C. (2009). Continuing bonds, risk factors for complicated grief, and adjustment to bereavement. *Death Studies*, *34*(1), 1–29.

Frankl, V. E. (1985). *Man's search for meaning*. New York: Simon and Schuster.

Freeman, M. (2014). *The priority of the other*. New York: Oxford University Press.

Geiger, M. (1986). *The significance of art: A phenomenological approach to aesthetics*. Lanham, MD: University Press of America.

Germer, C., Siegel, R. D., and Fulton, P. R. (Eds.). (2016). *Mindfulness and psychotherapy*. New York: Guilford Press.

Ginwright, S. (2015). *Hope and healing in urban education: How urban activists and teachers are reclaiming matters of the heart*. London: Routledge.

Given, L. M. (2008). *The Sage encyclopedia of qualitative research methods*. Thousand Oaks, CA: Sage.

Gross, P. L., and Shapiro, S. I. (1996). Characteristics of the Taoist sage in Chuang-Tzu and the creative photographer. *Journal of Transpersonal Psychology*, *28*, 175–92.

Halkola, U. (2009). A photograph as a therapeutic experience. *European Journal of Psychotherapy and Counselling*, *11*(1), 21–33.

Harper, D. (2002). Talking about pictures: A case for photo elicitation. *Visual studies*, *17*(1), 13–26.

Harrison, B. (2009). Editor's introduction: Researching lives and the lived experience. *Life story research*, 1. Thousand Oaks, CA: Sage.

Hebert, R. S., Prigerson, H. G., Schulz, R., and Arnold, R. M. (2006). Preparing caregivers for the death of a loved one: A theoretical framework and suggestions for future research. *Journal of Palliative Medicine*, 9(5), 1164–71.

Hibberd, R. (2013). Meaning reconstruction in bereavement: Sense and significance. *Death Studies*, 37(7), 670–92.

Hochberg, T. (2003, April, May, June). Touching souls: Healing with bereavement photography. *Forum*, 6.

Holmes, J. (2014). *John Bowlby and attachment theory*. New York: Routledge.

Husserl, E. (1982). *Ideas pertaining to a pure phenomenology and to a phenomenological philosophy* (F. Kersten, trans.). The Hague, Netherlands: Martinus Nijhoff.

Jakoby, N. R. (2012). Grief as a social emotion: theoretical perspectives. *Death Studies*, 36(8), 679–711.

Jones, M. (2019, Dec. 19). The movement to bring death closer. *New York Times*. https://www.nytimes.com/2019/12/19/magazine/home-funeral.html?smid=nytcore-ios-share&referringSource=articleShare.

Kabat-Zinn, J. (1990). *Full catastrophe living: Using the wisdom of your body and mind to face stress, pain, and illness*. New York: Delacorte Press.

Kabat-Zinn, J. (2003). Mindfulness-based interventions in context: Past, present, and future. *Clinical Psychology: Science and Practice*, 10(2), 144–56.

Kabat-Zinn, J. (2004). *Wherever you go, there you are: Mindfulness meditation in everyday life*. New York: Hyperion.

Kim, J.-H. (2016). *Understanding narrative inquiry: The crafting and analysis of stories as research*. Thousand Oaks, CA: Sage.

Kirova, A., and Emme, M. (2006). Using photography as a means of phenomenological seeing: "Doing phenomenology" with immigrant children. *Indo-Pacific Journal of Phenomenology: Methodology: Special Edition*, 6, 1–12.

Klass, D., Silverman, P. R., and Nickman, S. L. (1996). *Continuing bonds: New understandings of grief*. Washington, DC: Taylor & Francis.

Knowles, J. G., and Cole, A. L. (2007). *Handbook of the arts in qualitative research: Perspectives, methodologies, examples, and issues*. Thousand Oaks, CA: Sage.

Kohut, M. (2011). Making art from memories: Honoring deceased loved ones through a scrapbooking bereavement group. *Art Therapy*, 28(3), 123–31.

Kornfield, J. (1993). *A path with heart: A guide through the perils and promises of spiritual life*. New York: Bantam Books.

Lazar, S. W., Kerr, C. E., Wasserman, R. H., Gray, J. R., Greve, D. N., Treadway, M. T., et al. (2005). Meditation experience is associated with increased cortical thickness. *Neuroreport*, 16(17), 1893.

Levine, S. (1987). *Healing into life and death*. Garden City, NY: Anchor/Doubleday.

Lister, S., Pushkar, D., and Connolly, K. (2008). Current bereavement theory: Implications for art therapy practice. *The Arts in Psychotherapy*, 35(4), 245–50. doi: 10.1016/j.aip.2008.06.006

Lobb, E. A., Kristjanson, L. J., Aoun, S. M., Monterosso, L., Halkett, G. K., and Davies, A. (2010). Predictors of complicated grief: A systematic review of empirical studies. *Death Studies*, 34(8), 673–98.

Loewenthal, D. (2013). Introducing phototherapy and therapeutic photography in a digital age. *Phototherapy and Therapeutic Photography in a Digital Age*, 5–20.

Lowey, S. E. (2008). Letting go before a death: A concept analysis. *Journal of Advanced Nursing*, 63(2), 208–15.

McBee, L. (2009). Mindfulness-based elder care: Communicating mindfulness to frail elders and their caregivers. In F. Didonna (ed.), *Clinical handbook of mindfulness* (pp. 431–45). New York: Springer.

McCarthy, J. R., Woodthorpe, K., and Almack, K. (2023). The aftermath of death in the continuing lives of the living: extending 'bereavement' paradigms through family and relational perspectives. *Sociology*, 57(6), 1356–74..

MacKinnon, C. J., Smith, N. G., Henry, M., Milman, E., Berish, M., Farrace, A., and Cohen, S. R. (2016). A pilot study of meaning-based group counseling for bereavement. *OMEGA-Journal of Death and Dying*, 72(3), 210–33.

McGoldrick, M., and Hardy, K. V. (Eds.). (2008). *Re-visioning family therapy: Race, culture, and gender in clinical practice*. New York: Guilford Press.

Meraud, T. (2010). More than meets the eye: Connections between phenomenology and art. *Postgraduate Journal of Aesthetics*, 7(3), 25–35.

McNiff, S. (2011). Artistic expressions as primary modes of inquiry. *British Journal of Guidance & Counselling*, 39(5), 385–96. http://dx.doi.org/ 10.1080/03069885.2011.621526.

Merleau-Ponty, M., Davis, O., and Baldwin, T. (2004). *The world of perception*. London: Cambridge University Press.

Moran, D. (2002). *Introduction to phenomenology*. New York: Taylor & Francis.

Moustakas, C. (1994). *Phenomenological research methods*. Thousand Oaks, CA: Sage.

Natoli, A., and Suler, J. (2011). The psychologically beneficial aspects of photography. Unpublished manuscript, Department of Psychology, Rider University, Lawrenceville, NJ.

Neimeyer, R. A. (2016). Meaning reconstruction in the wake of loss: Evolution of a research program. *Behaviour Change*, 33(2), 65–79.

Nieberding, W. J. (2011). Photography, phenomenology and sight: Toward an understanding of photography through the discourse of vision (Doctoral dissertation, Ohio State University, Columbia, OH).

Padma, J. H. (2021). *Field of blessings: Ritual & consciousness in the work of buddhist healers*. United Kingdom: John Hunt Publishing.

Pietkiewicz, I., and Smith, J. A. (2014). A practical guide to using Interpretative Phenomenological Analysis in qualitative research psychology. *Czasopismo Psychologiczne/ Psychological Journal*, 20(1), 7–14.

Pimenta, S., and Poovaiah, R. (2010). On defining visual narratives. *IDC Design Research Journal*, 3, 25–46.

Pole, C. (2004). *Seeing is believing? Approaches to visual research*. Bingley, United Kingdom: Emerald Group.

Rinpoche, S., Gaffney, P., and Harvey, A. (1994). *The Tibetan book of living and dying*. New York: HarperCollins.

Rockwell, D., and Valle, R. (2016). Mindfulness as therapy: How Buddhist psychology contributes to enhancing therapist efficacy and client outcomes. *The Changing Faces of Therapy: Evolving Perspectives in Clinical Practice and Assessment*, 320–60.

Rolland, J. S. (2004). Helping families with anticipatory loss and terminal illness. *Living Beyond Loss: Death in the Family*, 2, 213–36.

Ruby, J. (1995). *Secure the shadow: Death and photography in America*. Cambridge, MA: MIT Press.

Rumi, J. A., and Nicholson, R. A. (2004). *Silent words: A Selection of poetry and prose of mowlavi*. Tehran: Hermes.

Rummet, H. (2006). *Pathways of the soul: Exploring the human journey*. Victoria, BC, Canada: Trafford.

Rushton, C. H., Sellers, D. E., Heller, K. S., Spring, B., Dossey, B. M., and Halifax, J. (2009). Impact of a contemplative end-of-life training program: Being with dying. *Palliative and Supportive Care*, 7(4), 405–14.

Ryan, J., and Molesey, E. (2012). Photography as a tool of awareness. *Journal of Transpersonal Psychology*, 44(1), 92–97.

Salmon, J. R., Kwak, J., Acquaviva, K. D., Brandt, K., and Egan, K. A. (2005). Transformative aspects of caregiving at life's end. *Journal of Pain and Symptom Management*, 29(2), 121–29.

Salzberg, S. (1999). *Heart as wide as the world: Stories on the path of lovingkindness* [New ed.]. Boston: Shambhala.

Sas, C., and Coman, A. (2016). Designing personal grief rituals: An analysis of symbolic objects and actions. *Death Studies*, 40(9), 558–69.

Schulz, R., Hebert, R., and Boerner, K. (2008). Bereavement after caregiving. *Geriatrics*, 63(1), 20.

Shirai, Y., Silverberg Koerner, S., and Baete Kenyon, D. Y. (2009). Reaping caregiver feelings of gain: The roles of socio-emotional support and mastery. *Aging and Mental Health*, 13(1), 106–17.

Suler, J. R. (2011). "Mindfulness in Photography." In R. Zakia (ed.), *Perception and Imaging*, 4th edition (pp. 235–39). Oxford: Focal Press (Elsevier).

Surya, D. (1997). *Awakening the Buddha within; Eight steps to enlightenment: Tibetan wisdom for the Western world*. New York, NY: Broadway Books.

Thomas, J. N. (2016). Mindful photography and its implications in end-of-life caregiving: An art-based phenomenology (Doctoral dissertation, Sofia University).

Thomas, J. (2021). Mindful Photography. In *New Techniques of Grief Therapy* (pp. 201–204). New York: Routledge.

Trungpa, C. (2008). *True perception*. Boston: Shambhala.

Torges, C. M., Stewart, A. J., and Nolen-Hoeksema, S. (2008). *Regret resolution, aging, and adapting to loss. Psychology and Ageing*, 23(1), 169–80.

Valle, R., and Floyd, N. (2017). Psychology of devotion and devotional experience: A developmental perspective. *The Humanistic Psychologist*, 45(2), 109–21.

Valle, R., and Mohs, M. (1998). Transpersonal awareness in phenomenological inquiry. In W. Braud and R. Anderson (eds.), *Transpersonal research methods for the social sciences* (pp. 95–113). Thousand Oaks, CA: Sage.

Valle, R., & Mohs, M. (2006). *Opening to dying and grieving: A sacred journey.* St. Paul, MN: YES International.

Van Puymbroeck, M., Payne, L. L., and Hsieh, P.-C. (2007). A phase I feasibility study of yoga on the physical health and coping of informal caregivers. *Evidence-Based Complementary and Alternative Medicine*, 4(4), 519–29.

Walsh, R., and Vaughan, F. (1993). *Paths beyond ego: The transpersonal vision.* New York: Penguin.

Walsh, R. (2008). *Spiritual resources in family therapy.* New York: Guilford Press.

Weiser, J. (2018). *Phototherapy Techniques: Exploring the Secrets of Personal Snapshots and Family Albums.* New York: Routledge.

White, M. (1963). Equivalence: The perenial trend. *PSA Journal*, 29(7), 17–21.

White, M., Bunnell, P. C., Pellerano, M. B., and Rauch, J. B. (1989). *Minor White: The eye that shapes.* Princeton, NJ: Princeton University Art Museum.

Zakia, R. D. (2013). *Perception and imaging: Photography—a way of seeing.* Burlington, MA: Focal Press.

INDEX

About the Author

Dr. Jessica Thomas holds an MS in Marriage and Family Therapy and a PhD in Psychology with an emphasis in Transpersonal Psychology. She is a therapist, clinical supervisor, grief educator, and organizational consultant.

Jessica has served on the not-for-profit board of the NW Association for Death Education and Bereavement Support for over eight years. She has been a hospice volunteer and a proud volunteer and advocate for Death Cafes, working to increase awareness of death and dying in the greater community.

As a professor at Lewis & Clark College, she has created coursework and taught on death and grief, psycho-spiritual development and counseling, research methods, and clinical supervision. She also provides clinical supervision for counseling students at the California Institute of Integral Studies. Her doctoral research, *Mindful Photography and Its Implications in End-of-Life Caregiving: An Art-based Phenomenology*, focused on creative expression and the experience of anticipatory loss. Jessica's subsequent developments include integrating her mindful photography therapeutic method into groups. Within and Without Mindful

Photography reflection groups support those who are traversing grief due to a death or other major life transition.

She offers both professional and community workshops, presentations, and talks on death and grief, transpersonal psychology, and the Within and Without Method. Some of Jessica's favorite projects involve consulting with organizations and developing death and grief education, as well as facilitating creative training sessions and meaningful group practices.

www.ingramcontent.com/pod-product-compliance
Lightning Source LLC
Chambersburg PA
CBHW070346270326
41926CB00017B/4018